Bender

HIGH SPEED SAILING

HIGH SPEED SAILING

DESIGN FACTORS

A Study of High-Performance Multihull Yacht Design

JOSEPH NORWOOD Jr, PhD

DODD, MEAD & COMPANY · NEW YORK

Published in the United States of America
by Dodd, Mead & Company, Inc., 1979

ISBN: 0-396-07738-2

Library of Congress Catalog Card Number: 79-87640

Designed by Jonathan Sharp

Printed in Great Britain

CONTENTS

INTRODUCTION

The origins of man's use of wind-driven water craft are lost in antiquity. With the coming of the industrial revolution in the nineteenth century and the availability of cheap fuels, sail was overtaken on the commercial ocean routes of the world in the late 1800's and the massive government-funded research effort on ships withdrew its interest from sail. With only minor exceptions, the primary use of sailing craft since that time has been for sporting purposes and many of their design concepts are nineteenth century ones.

The period between the twilight of sailing ships and the present has witnessed a scientific and technological expansion on a vast scale. Aviation has progressed from its frail beginnings to the present supersonic jet aeroplanes, and our knowledge of aerodynamics is nearly complete over a vast range of speeds. The space effort has led to the development of new materials having many times the specific strength of steel. As a result, the scientific and technical know-how and the state of materials technology allow us to improve the efficiency of sailing craft greatly over their present configuration.

In the commercial ship sizes, adequate stability is available with a conventional single-hulled configuration for an improvement in sail rigs and sail handling machinery to give us ships that could make a good profit for their owners in this age of decreasing oil supplies. We shall not be concerned with high-performance vessels in these sizes however, but shall instead concentrate on yacht size craft from daysailers to 100 feet or so. In these sizes, multihull unballasted craft have a clear performance advantage over monohull ballasted yachts. The design of high-performance multihulls and the quantitative affect of various design parameters on the performance of the boat are the subjects of this book.

A lot has been written about boats from a qualitative or empirical point of view; very few treatments have been done that were useful in a quantitative way. There is much experience available in monohulls, but some of the basic lessons with multihulls are still being learned the hard way. The reason that the sailing problem has not been solved in a general way is that first, it is a very difficult problem to specify, and second, even if you can specify the problem adequately, it is nonlinear and cannot be solved exactly in an analytical fashion. It vii should be said, however, that owing to their relative lack of heeling, multihulls are more amenable to analysis than monohulls.

This book is rather technical and contains numerous equations, but with the sole exception of the section on hull resistance, the level of the mathematics does not go beyond simple algebra and the occasional bit of trigonometry. The mathematics is really included for confidence and completeness. Conclusions drawn from its use are discussed and presented in tabular form, and lavish use is made of line drawings and diagrams. The book is intended for serious study, but a lack of comfort with equations will not prevent the reader from appreciating the qualitative arguments based upon the equations or the tabulated quantitative data.

The book opens with a discussion of the basic nature of wind-driven water craft. In the chapters that follow, the effect of the various components of the boat on its overall performance are examined. In chapter 8 the problem is considered from a more general point of view and quantitative predictions of boat speed as a function of wind strength and direction and the basic parameters of the boat are derived. In the closing chapters, the various multihull types are considered in some detail and some concrete ideas are put forth for their development. An extensive bibliography is given and the book is thoroughly indexed. In addition, you will find in Appendix D that all symbols are defined and indexed according to the equation in which they first occur.

The author would like to acknowledge his indebtedness to numerous correspondents in England and the US. Special thanks go to Dick Newick who read the manuscript and made valuable suggestions for its improvement and Cdr. George Chapman, RN who loaned his hydrofoil proa *Tiger* to me during my stay in England. I should also mention Michael Ellison and John Morwood in England and Harry Morss, Jack Shortall and Walter Castles in the US who have contributed notably to my education. The publications of the Amateur Yacht Research Society have been the source of much stimulation and inspiration in the development of my ideas. Finally, but far from least, I should like to express my loving thanks to my wife, Frances, who typed the manuscript and provided the environment for its creation.

Oriental, N.C.   Joseph Norwood, Jr.
February, 1979

1 THE PHYSICS OF FAST SAILING

Sailing boats exploit the discontinuity in fluid flow that exists at the air/water interface in order to propel themselves. We may consider the water to be at rest and describe the velocity of the wind by a vector $\mathbf{V}_T$. The magnitude of this vector is equal to the wind speed with respect to the water and the direction of the vector coincides with the wind direction. Under the influence of the wind, the boat moves at a speed V_B in a direction given by the vector $\mathbf{V}_B$. Motion of any object through still air with a velocity $\mathbf{V}_B$ gives rise to an induced wind velocity $-\mathbf{V}_B$ in the opposite direction, hence the total or apparent wind velocity felt by the boat is the vector sum of the true and induced winds, that is

$$\mathbf{V}_A = \mathbf{V}_T - \mathbf{V}_B. \tag{1-1}$$

This vector equation can be represented schematically by the triangle shown in Fig. 1-1. In this figure each of the sides of the triangle is given by a line whose length is proportional to the magnitude of the

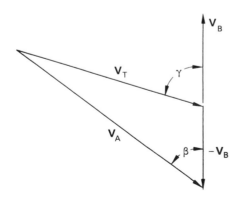

Fig. 1-1. The sailing triangle showing the apparent wind as the vector sum of the true wind and induced wind.

appropriate vector; the directions of the lines are those of the corresponding wind directions. These directions are described in the figure by the angles γ and β. The interior angle opposite the side V_A is $(180° - \gamma)$ and since the sum of the interior angles of any plane triangle is 180°, the angle between the vectors $\mathbf{V}_T$ and $\mathbf{V}_A$ must be $(\gamma - \beta)$.

This simple wind vector triangle can be used to derive a very useful relation. The law of sines in trigonometry states that the ratio of any side of a triangle to the sine of the opposite angle is a constant. Hence

$$\frac{V_T}{\sin \beta} = \frac{V_A}{\sin(180° - \gamma)} = \frac{V_B}{\sin(\gamma - \beta)}. \tag{1-2}$$

In terms of V_T and V_B, this gives

$$\frac{V_B}{V_T} = \frac{\sin(\gamma - \beta)}{\sin \beta} = \frac{\sin \gamma \cos \beta - \cos \gamma \sin \beta}{\sin \beta}$$

$$= \sin \gamma \ \text{ctn} \ \beta - \cos \gamma, \tag{1-3}$$

where $\cos \beta / \sin \beta = \text{ctn} \ \beta$ (the cotangent of β) varies with β as shown in Fig. 1-2.

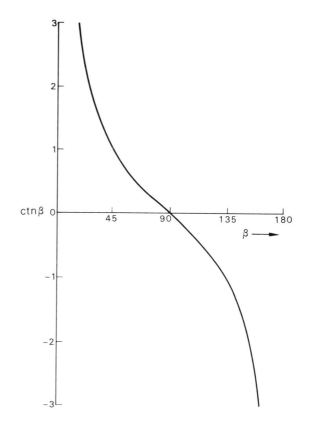

Fig. 1-2. Cotangent β as a function of β.

Note that Eq. (1-3) contains no approximation; it is simply an alternate statement of Eq. (1-1) and applies equally to any sort of body moving through air. Since V_T is known from a static measurement and the course angle to the true wind γ is known, we see that V_B is a function only of the angle β. In order to see what β is, we must now begin to describe sailing boats.

The essential elements for momentum transfer from the wind are a vertical aerofoil (sail) and a vertical hydrofoil (keel, centreboard, etc.) as shown in Fig. 1-3. In practice, the vertical downward force of

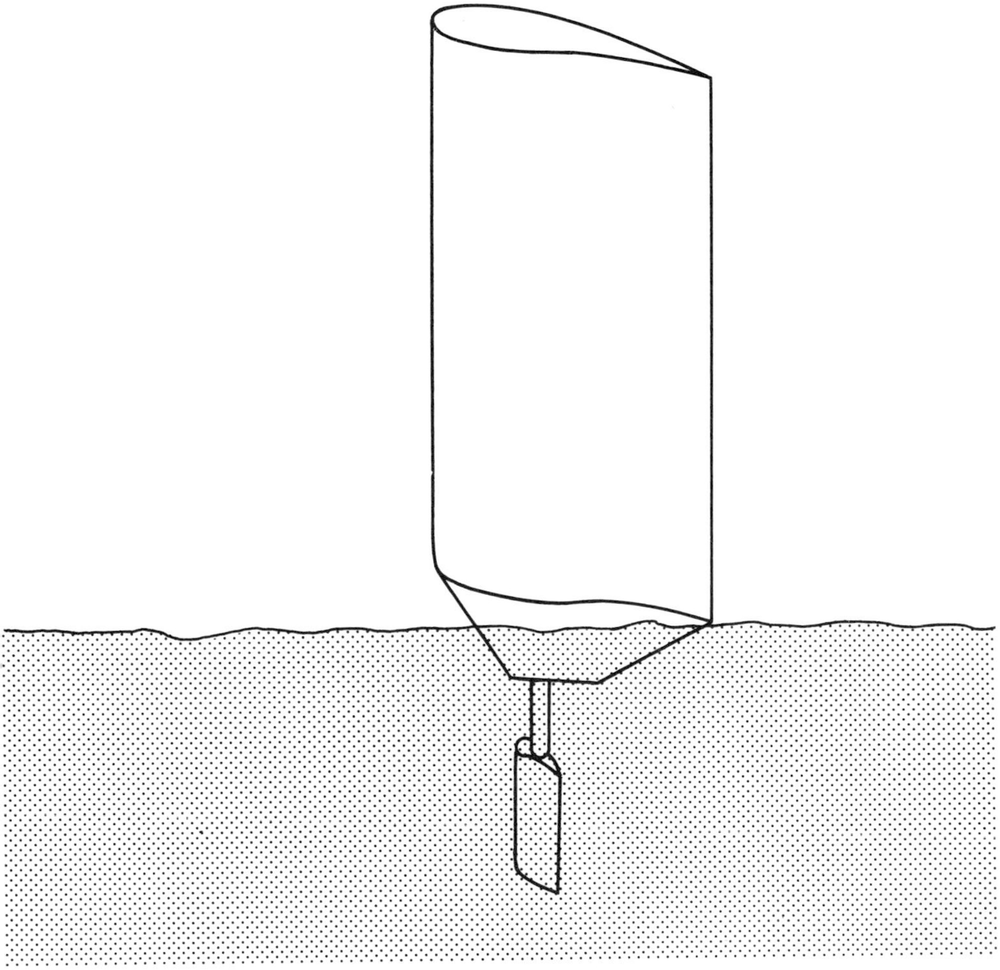

Fig. 1-3. The ideal yacht: essential elements for momentum transfer.

gravity requires the buoyant support of a hull or hulls. These hulls do not play any role in the momentum transfer in the limit where the hydrofoil function is wholly fulfilled by a keel or board. In the horizontal plane, the foils shown from above in Fig. 1-4(a) give rise to the forces indicated in Fig. 1-4(b). The water flow $-V_B$ over the hydrofoil and the airflow V_A over the aerofoil produce forces F_H and F_A respectively. In order that the boat be in equilibrium (unaccelerated)

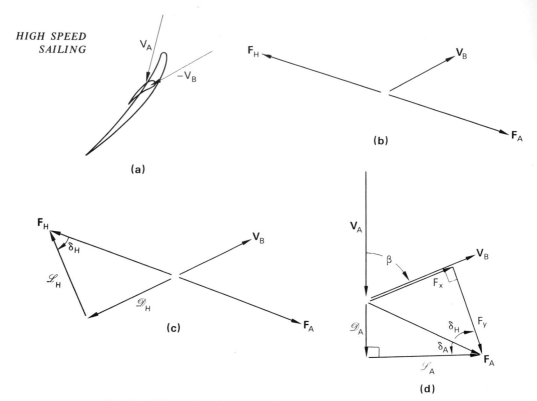

Fig. 1-4. Illustrating the course theorem.

$$F_H = F_A. \tag{1-4}$$

The force $\mathbf{F}_H$ generated by the hydrofoil can be decomposed into a component of drag in the $-V_B$ direction $\mathscr{D}_H$ and a component of lift at right angles to the course, $\mathscr{L}_H$, as shown in Fig. 1-4(c). The angle $\delta_H = \mathrm{arcctn}(\mathscr{L}_H/\mathscr{D}_H)$ is the *hydrodynamic drag angle*. The aerodynamic vector $\mathbf{F}_A$ can be decomposed into components parallel and perpendicular to $\mathbf{V}_B$: F_x, the driving force in the direction of the motion and F_y, the sideforce. It can also be decomposed parallel and perpendicular to $\mathbf{V}_A$ as the aerodynamic drag $\mathscr{D}_A$ and aerodynamic lift $\mathscr{L}_A$ for which the *aerodynamic drag angle* $\delta_A = \mathrm{arcctn}(\mathscr{L}_A/\mathscr{D}_A)$ can be defined. These two decompositions are shown in Fig. 1-4(d). Since $F_x = \mathscr{D}_H$ and $F_y = \mathscr{L}_H$, thus the angle between $\mathbf{F}_A$ and $\mathbf{F}_y$ is δ_H. The lift $\mathscr{L}_A$ is perpendicular to $\mathbf{V}_A$ and $\mathbf{F}_y$ is perpendicular to V_B; thus the angle between $\mathscr{L}_A$ and $\mathbf{F}_y$ must be equal to the angle between $\mathbf{V}_A$ and $\mathbf{V}_B$, that is

$$\beta = \delta_H + \delta_A. \tag{1-5}$$

This relation, known as the *course theorem*, and the definitions

$$\begin{aligned} \delta_H &= \mathrm{arcctn}\ \mathscr{L}_H/\mathscr{D}_H, \\ \delta_A &= \mathrm{arcctn}\ \mathscr{L}_A/\mathscr{D}_A, \end{aligned} \tag{1-6}$$

of the drag angles constitute a mathematical description of a sailing boat.

We see from Eq. (1-3) that for values of γ not too near 180°, ctn β
should be as large as possible in order to provide a high value of V_B/V_T.
Figure 1-2 shows us that this corresponds to small values of β.
Equations (1-5) and (1-6) imply that the use of foils having large lift-
to-drag ratios will result in low values of β.

Clearly, the knowledge of δ_H and δ_A for all values of γ and V_T amounts
to a complete solution of the problem. The accurate calculation of the
lifts and drags for all V_T and γ is a complicated problem and the results
of any mathematical model are subject to question. For the purpose of
establishing a firm foundation to our basic design criteria, we shall look
at some measured drag angles for a broad spectrum of sailing craft
and try to draw some conclusions.

In Fig. 1-5 we have plotted the aero drag angle δ_A for an International
12-foot dinghy, a 12-metre boat, a Tornado catamaran, and an ice boat

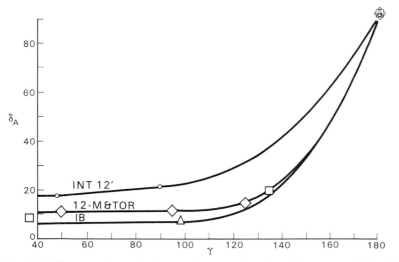

Fig. 1-5. The aerodynamic drag angle as a function of course angle to the
true wind.

as functions of the course angle γ. The data points taken from the table
on p. 313 of Ref. 1, are admittedly few and the choice of curves used to
fit them reflects my bias for a number 59 ship curve which I have
always found to fit physical data quite well.

The dinghy with its relatively low aspect ratio sail plan and high
parasitic wind resistance has the largest drag angle. The 12-metre boat
and the Tornado, both with high aspect ratio rigs and aerodynamically
'clean' decks have nearly identical values of δ_A for all γ. The ice boat,
using a fully battened unarig is somewhat more efficient.

Figure 1-6 shows a plot of the hydro drag angles δ_H for the same
boats. We see that the dinghy and the 12-metre boat have nearly
identical values of δ_H. This curve is very nearly linear and is a common
feature of all monohull sailing craft. The Tornado catamaran, typical
of fast multihulls, has a much lower value of δ_H and the ice boat with its
runners operating on 'rails' as it were, has an almost perfect curve with
$\delta_H \approx 0$ until a value of $\gamma \approx 180°$ is approached.

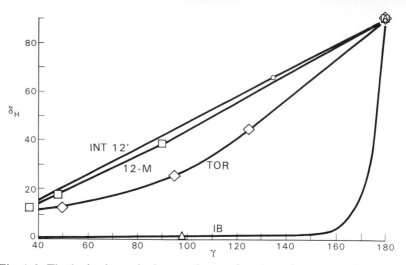

Fig. 1-6. The hydrodynamic drag angle as a function of course angle to the true wind.

Fig. 1-7. β versus γ for the International 12′ dinghy, a 12-metre yacht, a Tornado catamaran, and an ice boat.

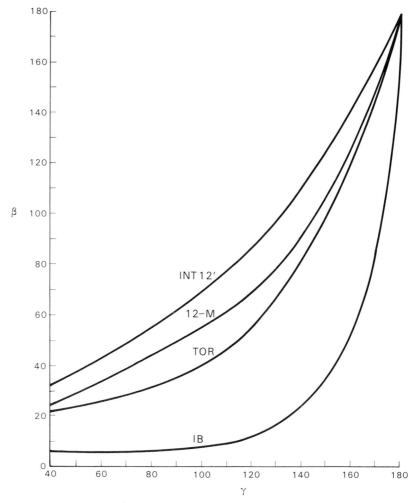

6

In order to give these data for drag angles some physical reality, we shall use their sum, $\delta_A + \delta_H = \beta$, shown plotted as a function of γ in Fig. 1-7, and Eq. (1-3) to compare V_B/V_T for our sample sailing craft. This comparison is shown in the form of polar plots of V_B/V_T versus γ with γ increasing ccw from the horizontal. In Fig. 1-8 the dinghy, the 12-metre, and the catamaran are compared, and in Fig. 1-9, the catamaran and the iceboat are shown. As you can see, iceboating at 80 knots plus is another world altogether!

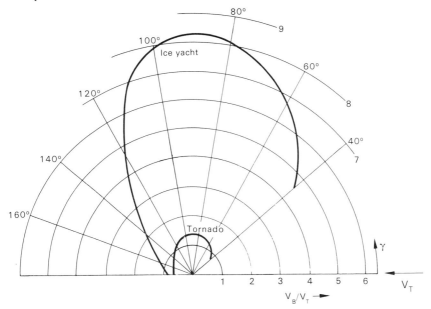

Fig. 1-8. Polar curves for the Tornado, 12-Metre, and International 12′ dinghy for $V_T \approx 10$ knots.

Fig. 1-9. Polar curves for the Tornado and the ice boat for $V_T \approx 10$ knots.

The main factor determining the aero drag angle is the ratio of sail area to parasitic (non lift-producing) area. In the case of the hydro drag angle, it is the leeway resistor area versus the area of the vertical

7

projection of the non lift-producing hull. In many cases these functions cannot be clearly separated, that is, the keel and hull are not distinct. This fact is a major complicating factor in attempting an analytical treatment.

For a given boat, these drag angles are a function not only of γ, the course angle, but also of V_T, the wind speed. The data given in Figs. 1-5 and 1-6 was taken for wind speeds in the 5-10 knot range. At higher wind speeds, heeling and the need to reduce sail area causes δ_A to increase and the effect of heeling and wind and motion induced waves causes δ_H to increase as well. Thus V_B/V_T decreases with increasing V_T as seen in Fig. 1-10 in which the polar plots of V_B/V_T for a 12-metre boat are compared for $V_T = 10$ and 20 knots.

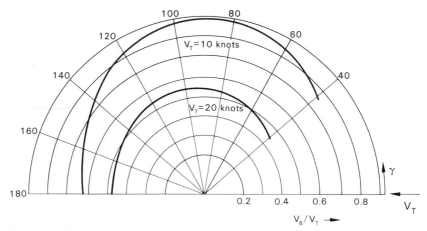

Fig. 1-10. Showing the decrease of V_B/V_T with increasing V_T for a 12-Metre yacht.

If we view the ideal yacht of Fig. 1-3 from dead ahead, (see Fig. 1-11) we see that the sideways components of the sail force F_y acting through the centre of effort of the sail and the lift exerted by the keel $\mathscr{L}_H = F_y$ lie in antiparallel directions along lines separated by a distance h. This forms a couple hF_y that tends to heel the boat to leeward. As the boat heels the couple formed by the shift of the centre of buoyancy to leeward with respect to the centre of gravity increases until it cancels the heeling torque:

$$hF_y = bW \tag{1-7}$$

where b is the horizontal distance between the centres of gravity and buoyancy. Since the heeling force F_y is proportional to the sail area, thus the maximum sail area that can be carried for a given apparent wind speed is proportional to the product of W and b/h. In the case of a heeled monohull as shown in Fig. 1-12, the distance b is small, hence the weight W must be large. In a boat like the 12-metre, this weight is carried in the form of lead at the bottom of the keel. In the case of the dinghy, crew shift to windward provides the righting moment.

Multihulls such as the catamaran shown in Fig. 1-13 are unballasted and depend upon their large lateral spread and consequent large value of b for their righting moment. The maximum righting moment is

8

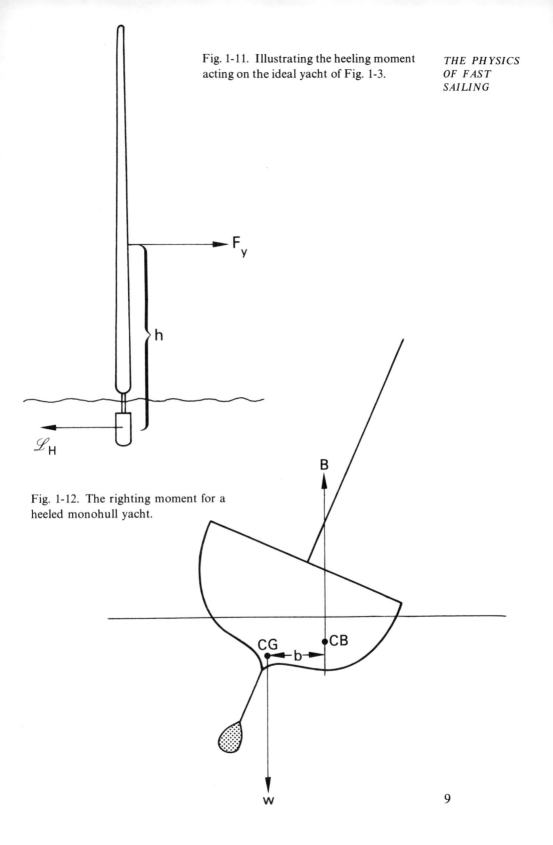

Fig. 1-11. Illustrating the heeling moment acting on the ideal yacht of Fig. 1-3.

F_y

h

$\mathscr{L}_H$

Fig. 1-12. The righting moment for a heeled monohull yacht.

B

CG •CB

←b→

w

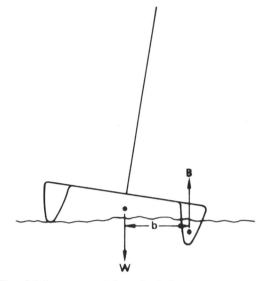

Fig. 1-13. The righting moment for a heeled catamaran.

achieved in a catamaran at a heel angle of 10° or less as compared to 30° or so for a monohull. Hence the effect on δ_A of the slightly greater relative parasitic drag area of the Tornado is compensated by the greater effective sail area associated with the lower angle of heel. For speed under sail, it is clear that multihulls are the way to go.

Multihull sailing craft may employ any of three possible hull configurations: a double outrigger or trimaran, a reversible single outrigger or proa, and a double canoe or catamaran. The trimaran consists of a central load-carrying hull stabilized by outriggers, one on either side. The proa has two dissimilar hulls. In order always to keep the heavy hull to windward, the proa must be able to sail in either direction. The catamaran features two similar hulls separated by a distance of about half the boat length.

In the following chapters we shall discuss in some detail the principles involved in the design of high speed sailing craft. In this discussion we shall constantly bear in mind the basic criterion for fast sailing craft as developed above, namely that the aerodynamic and hydrodynamic lift-to-drag ratios should be as large as possible for various sized craft sailed in sheltered and offshore waters.

REFERENCES

1 Bruce, Edmond and Harry Morss, *Design for Fast Sailing*, (AYRS 82), Hermitage, Berks.: Amateur Yacht Research Society, 1976.

2 Marchaj, C. A., *Sailing, Theory and Practice*, Adlard Coles Ltd and Dodd, Mead & Co., 1964.

3 Marchaj, C. A., *Forms of Sailing—Factors Affecting Yacht Performance—High Speed Sailing*. Land's End Publishing Corp., 1973.

2 HULLS AND OUTRIGGERS

The primary purpose of a boat hull is to provide a vertical buoyant force in opposition to the weight of the boat and accommodation for the crew and cargo. The motion of the hull through the water gives rise to a resistive drag R that constitutes by far the largest part of the hydrodynamic drag $\mathscr{D}_K$. Therefore a knowledge of the nature of this resistance as a means to minimizing it is of prime importance to the design of really fast sailing boats.

The parameters that enter into the description of a hull and its motion through the water are:

V_B, the speed of the boat through the water, ft/sec
W, the weight of the loaded hull equal to the weight of the water displaced, lbs.
L, the waterline length, ft
B, the waterline beam, ft
G_m, the girth of the largest underwater cross section, ft

The resistance experienced by a non-planing displacement-type hull is mainly due to frictional momentum exchange with the viscous water and to effects associated with the presence of the air/water surface. The frictional part of the resistance has been found to obey the relation

$$R_F = \tfrac{1}{2}\rho_H V_B^2 A_w C_F \tag{2-1}$$

where ρ_H is the mass density of the water ($\tfrac{1}{2}\rho_H = 0.996$ slug/ft^3), A_w is the total wetted area of the hull, and C_F is the friction coefficient. This latter quantity is determined by the interplay between inertial and viscous forces in the boundary layer and is expressable as a function of a dimensionless parameter known as the Reynolds' number

$$\mathrm{Re} = \frac{\rho_H V_B L}{\eta} \tag{2-2}$$

where η is the viscosity. For seawater and V_B expressed in knots (1 knot = 1.69 ft/s),

$$\mathrm{Re} = 1.27 \cdot 10^5 V_B L. \tag{2-3}$$

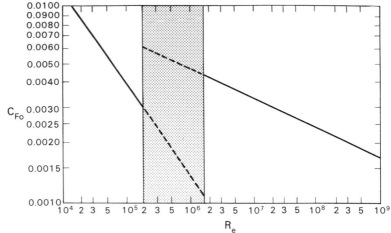

Fig. 2-1. The friction coefficient as a function of Reynolds number.

In Fig. 2-1, the functional relationship between C_{Fo} and Re is shown. For Re less than $2 \cdot 10^5$, laminar flow prevails and the ideal friction coefficient is given by the Blasius formula

$$C_{Fo} = \frac{1.369}{\sqrt{\text{Re}}} \qquad (2\text{-}4)$$

In the shaded region between Re $= 2 \cdot 10^5$ and Re $= 1.5 \cdot 10^6$, the flow is in transition from laminar to turbulent flow. Large eddies are present and the value of C_{Fo} is subject to sizeable fluctuations. For values of Re greater than $1.5 \cdot 10^6$, fully developed turbulent flow is established and C_{Fo} is given by the Schoenherr formula

$$C_{Fo} = \frac{0.472}{(\log_{10} \text{Re})^{2.58}} . \qquad (2\text{-}5)$$

This condition is satisfied for $V_B L$ greater than 12 knots-feet and so applies for all motion of interest in full size hulls. It has been found that the theoretical coefficient C_{Fo} must be amended somewhat for use in Eq. (2-1). The empirical expression for C_F is therefore

$$C_F = (C_{Fo} + 0.0005)\left[1 + 1.5\left(\frac{B+H}{2L}\right)^{1.5} + 7\left(\frac{B+H}{2L}\right)^3\right] \qquad (2\text{-}6)$$

which accurately describes the drag experienced by a real hull with realistic finish and inevitable flow separations near the stern.

The other major component of hull drag that we shall call the *wave drag* can be described in a qualitative way as follows. Bernoulli's law requires that the height, ζ, of the water along the hull with respect to the static waterline and the speed of the water past the hull, V, obey the relation

$$V^2 + 2g\zeta = V_B^2 \qquad (2\text{-}7)$$

12   where $g = 32.17$ ft/s^2 is the acceleration of gravity. The water is slowed

at the bow of the boat (hence $\zeta > 0$), accelerates to a speed slightly in excess of V_B as the flow expands past the section of maximum area ($\zeta < 0$), and is slowed near the stern ($\zeta > 0$) in order for the flow to merge with the wake. Thus a pattern of divergent bow and stern waves are generated in addition to a transverse wave associated with water displaced vertically. It is a property of gravity waves in deep water that the propagation speed of the wave V_W is proportional to the square root of the wavelength λ. Since the waves must move with the boat, we have

$$V_B = V_W = \sqrt{\frac{\lambda g}{2\pi}}, \qquad (2\text{-}8)$$

thus the wavelength increases as $V_B{}^2$. This leads to the situation shown in Fig. 2-2. (If the finite depth of the water d is taken into account,

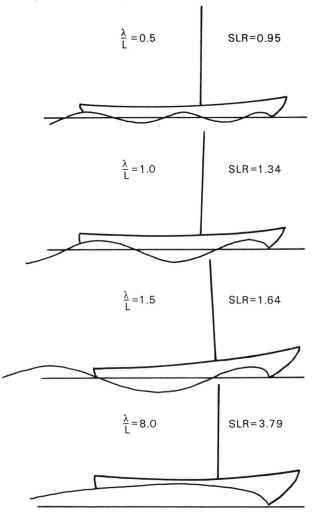

$\frac{\lambda}{L} = 0.5$ SLR=0.95

$\frac{\lambda}{L} = 1.0$ SLR=1.34

$\frac{\lambda}{L} = 1.5$ SLR=1.64

$\frac{\lambda}{L} = 8.0$ SLR=3.79

Fig. 2-2. The nature of wave drag.

then $V_B = \sqrt{\dfrac{\lambda g}{2\pi}} \cdot \sqrt{\tanh \dfrac{2\pi d}{\lambda}}$ which for d much less than λ tends to $V_B = \sqrt{gd}$. At about this speed in shallow water, frictional momentum exchange with the bottom begins to make itself felt). In Fig. 2-2 we have sketched the bow wave system associated with the motion for several different speeds. Using Eq. (2-8), we may express the speed in a non-dimensional form as the ratio of wavelength λ to boat length L

$$F = \frac{V_B}{\sqrt{gL}} = \frac{1}{\sqrt{2\pi}}\sqrt{\frac{\lambda}{L}}, \qquad (2\text{-}9)$$

where F is the *Froude number*. Naval architects often express the Froude number in an alternate form as the speed in knots divided by the square root of the length in feet. This is called the speed-length ratio (SLR) and it is related to F by a constant: $\text{SLR}/F = 3.36$. We see that for $\lambda \approx L$ up to $\lambda = 3L$ or $4L$, the average slope of the water on which the boat is sailing is positive and the boat thus finds itself sailing uphill on its own bow wave. If, for a simple example, the bow wave profile can be described as

$$z = \zeta \cos kx \qquad (2\text{-}10)$$

where

$$k = \frac{2\pi}{\lambda} = \frac{g}{V_B{}^2}, \qquad (2\text{-}11)$$

then the slope of the wave is $-\zeta k \sin kx$ and the average slope experienced by a boat of length L is

$$\frac{\Delta z}{\Delta x} = \begin{cases} \dfrac{\zeta}{L}\left(1 - \cos \dfrac{1}{F^2}\right); & F^2 \geq \dfrac{1}{2\pi} \\[2ex] 0; & F^2 < \dfrac{1}{2\pi} \end{cases} \qquad (2\text{-}12)$$

The wave resistance is just the component of the weight lying along the slope, $W \sin \theta$, which for the small slopes experienced by lean hulls equals $W \tan \theta = W(\Delta z/\Delta x)$. Thus

$$R_W \approx \frac{W\zeta}{L}\left(1 - \cos \frac{1}{F^2}\right) \qquad (2\text{-}13)$$

A similar equation was derived empirically by Piper Mason who found that it provided a good fit to monohull data.

We can estimate the magnitude of ζ, the bow wave amplitude as follows. The water is pushed aside a distance proportional to B in a time proportional to L/V_B, thus the average speed of the displaced water is $V_B(B/L)$. Equating the corresponding kinetic energy $(W/2g)V_B{}^2(B/L)^2$ to the gravitational potential $(W/g)g\zeta$, we find that

$$\zeta \propto \frac{V_B{}^2}{g}\left(\frac{B}{L}\right)^2, \qquad (2\text{-}14)$$

hence

$$R_W \approx WF^2 \left(\frac{B}{L}\right)^2 \left(1 - \cos \frac{1}{F^2}\right) \tag{2-15}$$

represents a zero-order approximation for the wave resistance. This is not good enough for our purposes, however.

An exact theory was given by Havelock in 1932. A simplified, but still quite general form of Havelock's equation has been found by Castles for hulls with lateral and longitudinal symmetry. A discussion of the physical basis of Havelock's theory and Castle's equations for single or multiple hulls is given in Appendix A. Castles' equation for a single hull is

$$R_W = \tfrac{1}{2}\rho_H \left(\frac{\sigma}{L}\right)^2 V_B{}^2 C_W \tag{2-16}$$

where

$$C_W = \frac{4}{\pi C_P{}^2} \int_{x_0}^{\infty} (1 - \cos x) \frac{x^2 e^{-ax^2}\, dx}{\sqrt{x^2 - x_0{}^2}} \tag{2-17}$$

and

$$a = \frac{2\delta}{L}\left(\frac{F}{C_P}\right)^2; \qquad x_0 = C_P/F^2. \tag{2-18}$$

The quantity δ is the depth of the centroid of the maximum cross section for which σ is the area. The prismatic coefficient C_P is defined by

$$C_P = \frac{W}{\rho_H\, g \sigma L} \tag{2-19}$$

and therefore describes the distribution of cross sectional area along the length of the boat.

The wave resistance is more or less insensitive to the shape of the hull cross section. This is not true for the frictional resistance which depends directly upon the wetted surface area A_W. This quantity is given quite accurately (± 1 percent) for a wide variety of forms by

$$A_W = 0.74 G_m L \tag{2-20}$$

The minimum girth for a given enclosed area is featured by the semi-circular cross section for which $G_m = \tfrac{1}{2}\pi B$ and $A_W = 1.16BL$. Since the wave resistance is shape independent, we are free to concentrate our interest on semi-circular sections. For this case $\sigma = \pi B^2/8$, $\delta = B/\pi$, and the total resistance can be written in terms of the Froude number F, the length-to-beam ratio L/B, and the prismatic coefficient C_P as

$$\frac{R}{W} = \frac{1.48}{C_P} F^2 \left(\frac{L}{B}\right) C_F + \frac{1}{4}\frac{F^2}{C_P{}^3}\left(\frac{B}{L}\right)^2$$

$$\times \int_{C_P/F^2}^{\infty} (1 - \cos x) \frac{x^2 \exp\left(\dfrac{-2BF^2x^2}{\pi L C_P{}^2}\right) dx}{\sqrt{x^2 - (C_P/F^2)^2}} \tag{2-21}$$

15

One of the first numbers to be generated when planning a boat is the *displacement-length ratio* DLR $= \Delta/(.01L)^3$ where Δ is the displacement in long tons ($\Delta = W/2240$). Using Eq. (2-19), we find for semi-circular cross sections that

$$\text{DLR} = 1.12 \cdot 10^4 C_P \left(\frac{B}{L}\right)^2. \qquad (2-22)$$

In formulating a design, one is always limited by material strength-to-weight ratios and other factors to some minimum DLR. From Eq. (2-22) we see that an infinite variety of values of C_P and L/B correspond to a given DLR. The problem is to find the *best* set of values from the point of view of minimizing the total resistance. Both components of the resistance, friction and wave, increase with F^2, however the wave term also contains an additional function of F^2 that is

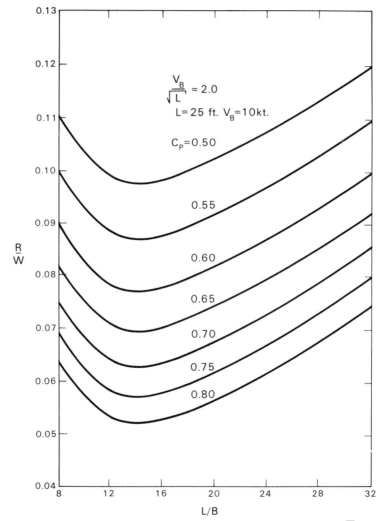

Fig. 2-3. Specific running resistance as a function of L/B for $V_B/\sqrt{L} = 2$.

zero for very small or very large value of F^2 and reaches a maximum value for $F^2 \approx 0.281(V_B/\sqrt{L} \approx 1.78)$. It therefore makes good sense to compare the resistance of hulls for this value of Froude number or one only slightly higher. We have calculated R/W using Eq. (2-21) for a range of prismatic coefficients from 0.50 to 0.80 and length-to-beam ratio from 8 to 32 at a fixed value of $F^2 = 0.355$ ($V_B/\sqrt{L} = 2.0$). The results are shown in Fig. 2-3. We see that higher prismatic coefficients are better than lower ones and that hulls in the L/B range from 12-16 are maximally efficient. The waterline length L has been taken as 25 feet in calculating the friction, however, the overall result is a very weak function of size, hence this choice does not limit the generality of these results.

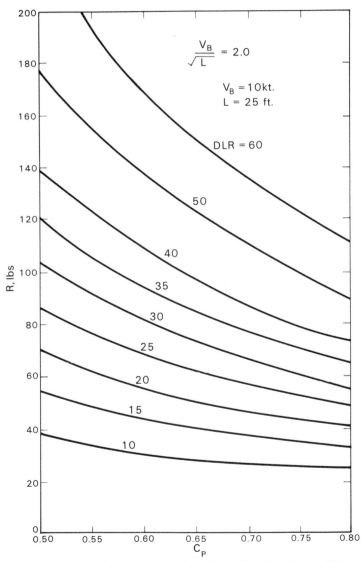

Fig. 2-4. Running resistance as a function of prismatic coefficient for $V_B/\sqrt{L} = 2.$

Interesting though it is, Fig. 2-3 still does not answer the basic question which is: for a given weight and length (DLR), what is the optimum value of prismatic coefficient in order that R (not R/W) be a minimum? This is answered by replotting the data as shown in Fig. 2-4. (The calculated values from which Figs. 2-3 and 2-4 were drawn are presented in tabular form in Appendix B.) The figure shows that high prismatics are best and, indeed implies that coefficients even higher than 0.80 are desirable. The choice of C_P is seen to be much less critical for the lower DLR's than for higher ones. In order to properly evaluate the data of Fig. 2-4, we must remember that eddy and flow separation effects owing to projections or small local radius of hull curvature are ignored. For high C_P, the hull tends to a scow shape (for which $C_P = 1.0$) and flow discontinuities at the bow can be expected to arise. These effects will tend to increase the resistance on the high C_P end of the curves. Thus it seems likely that the ideal value of C_P for the low-DLR hulls in which we are interested will lie in the range 0.65-0.75.

The effect of some variations from our standard hull (see Appendix A) for which the above results are derived should be noted. The effect of moving the cross section of maximum area forward of the midship position is an increase in the total resistance at all speeds. By moving the maximum section somewhat aft of amidships an average reduction of R/W by about 5 percent for $L/B = 12$ between the SLR values 0.8 to 3.0 is possible. Outside this speed range the logitudinally symmetrical hull is superior. The sensitivity of R/W to the position of the maximum section decreases with increasing L/B and C_P. For the high L/B, high C_P hulls of interest to us, placement of the maximum section can be dictated to a large extent by design factors other than resistance minimization.

Another possible modification is to broaden and flatten the sections of the after half of the hull. The effect of this on R/W is similar in magnitude and dependence on DLR to that of moving the maximum section aft. As in that case, stern flattening is disadvantageous for SLR's less than 0.8 and greater than 3.0. This modification also has the effect of damping pitching motion. The mechanism of this damping effect is discussed in some detail in Chapter 6. The pitching motion of low-DLR hulls is already highly damped even without stern flattening, thus proas pay only a marginal penalty for their longitudinal symmetry.

In order to make specific recommendations concerning the various multihull configurations, we must establish a working definition. We shall always refer to the weight-carrying hull as the *hull* and the float (or ama) as the *outrigger*. As a general rule, outriggers should be as light as possible and should not be used for stores and certainly not for accommodation.

A catamaran is a configuration of two identical hulls, or, in the case of assymetrical hulls, mirror images. In the daysailing sizes, catamarans are faster than trimarans owing to their ability to fly the windward hull and sail on one hull at a modest angle of heel. We shall discuss this question of hull flying further in Chapter 4. For catamarans to be sailed in relatively smooth waters, the hull sections should be semi-circular for most of the length with some flattening in the after third and a fairly rapid transition to elliptical, parabolic, and vee sections at the bow. For larger craft intended for offshore sailing, the drag that arises owing to the presence of ocean waves must be taken into account. This drag roughly doubles the effective resistance of a typical monohull racer sailing to windward in seas having a wavelength greater than the length of the boat. Rough water drag decreases with increasing L/B and is more or less insensitive to the beam-to-draught ratio B/H. This suggests that a practical optimum hull section for offshore use will correspond to B/H somewhat less than the semicircular value of 2. In rough water, large portions of the windward hull will be exiting and entering the water at high speed. In order to avoid pounding, the semi-circular section should be distorted into a rounded vee or parabolic section.

The question of whether to make catamaran hulls symmetrical or asymmetrical can be argued both ways. The intended purpose of an asymmetrical hull is, usually, to create horizontal lift on the more highly curved side. In the case of a catamaran with more or less flat outer sides and curved inner sides, the horizontal lift of the two hulls only serves to compress the cross beams unless heeling occurs. This is shown in Fig. 2-5. Only daysailers are sailed at such angles of heel and then only for short times. Even more discouraging to the notion of using hull asymmetry to enhance the lifting action of a long shallow hull is the fact that only for large angles of attack ($\gtrsim 10°$) does asymmetry make a significant contribution. Such a high angle of attack between the centreline of the boat and the course line would create an intolerable drag and is therefore out of the question. Asymmetric hulls have, however, been found to be highly resistant to broaching

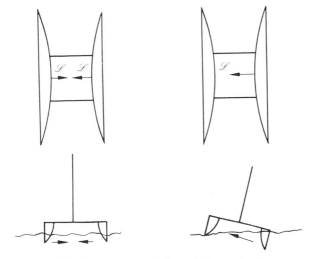

Fig. 2-5. The role of hull asymmetry in lateral lift production.

when running in heavy seas. This can be understood as shown in Fig. 2-6. When the boat, beginning to broach, reaches a yaw angle of 10° or so, the lift effect of the asymmetry in the leeward hull is strongly excited; the windward hull is at a negative angle of attack 19 and is not producing a significant lift. The lift of the leeward hull is accompanied by a large induced drag. The excess in drag of the leeward hull over the windward hull times the overall beam of the boat constitutes a torque to counter the broach. The superiority of asymmetrical hulls under these conditions is a matter of practical experience as well as theory. In making the decision of whether or not to use asymmetrical hulls, bear in mind that for a hull section having $B/H = 1.5$, a reasonable amount of asymmetry will cost a 5 percent increase in the wetted surface area and thus in frictional resistance. Friction is the dominant component of hull resistance when sailing in light airs (where multihulls are at a natural disadvantage anyway) and at very high speeds (SLR $\gtrsim 2.8$).

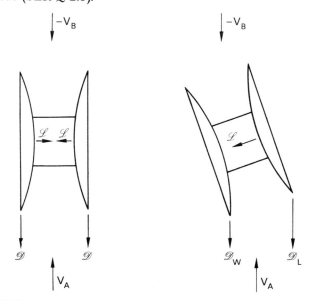

Fig. 2-6. Hull asymmetry as an anti-broaching feature.

The question of full, transom-type sterns or fine canoe-type sterns for catamarans where load carrying is not a major consideration can be settled in favour of the fine stern. At low speeds (SLR $\lesssim 1.8$) form drag acts against a full-sterned hull. The pressure of the water against the hull forward of the maximum section resulting in a resistive force is cancelled in a fine-sterned hull by the vector sum of the pressures aft of the maximum section except for a small amount that we lumped into the friction calculation [see Eq. (2-6)]. If the hull is terminated suddenly as is the case with full sterns, then this cancellation is not achieved. This is not the case in air where, for example, racing sports car bodies are found to give less resistance if the rear ends are chopped abruptly. At high speeds (SLR > 1.8) the difference between the resistance of full- and fine-sterned hulls is small with a slight advantage to the full stern. If we are considering an ocean racer, then we must take into account the fact that the sterns will often be buried in the seas that accompany high winds and fast sailing. Under these conditions, fine sterned hulls experience significantly less rough water drag.

20 Trimarans pose a different set of problems. Since all of the weight

is effectively carried by the central hull, this hull should have a semi-circular section over most of its length. This section may be somewhat flattened toward the stern and should be sharpened toward the bow. Since the DLR of the trimaran hull will be roughly twice that of either hull of a catamaran of similar overall specifications, it makes sense to use a transom stern. The transom should be narrow, however, and should not extend below the load water line.

The design of trimaran outriggers and their positioning with respect to the hull require special discussion. There are two schools of thought on the question of whether to fit full-buoyancy outriggers, either one of which can support the full weight of the craft without being driven under, or submersible outriggers that heel easily within a larger range of stable angles and give a better indication of when the boat is being over-driven. This question was settled (for me, at least) by a rash of capsizes in 1976-77 involving tris with low-buoyancy outriggers. It seems that when lying ahull in bad conditions, a wave may heel the trimaran in such a way as to drive the lee outrigger under. This outrigger having a high resistance to lateral motion then acts as a fixed pivot axis about which the boat can be capsized. The choice of low or full buoyancy outriggers is therefore the choice between the increased possibility of a wave capsize and the increased possibility of sailing the boat over. I personally feel that the latter is more acceptable.

For high performance, the outriggers should have semicircular sections over the after 70 percent of their length going over into a sharpening spade section toward the bow. In designing the outrigger and hull bows we want a configuration that will pierce small waves with minimum retardation and rise to large waves in order to avoid burying the bows with the possible consequence of a diagonal or stern-over-bow capsize. These requirements call for reasonably fine bows with moderate overhang and sheer, but little flare except in the main hull. The outrigger bows can be fitted with lifting plates as shown in Fig. 2-7.

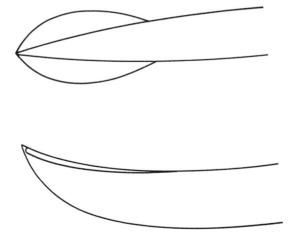

Fig. 2-7. Lift plates and sheer as dive preventors for outriggers.

In driving hard to windward, the deep running lee outrigger will generate a large resistance acting along a line to leeward of the driving force. The result is a torque that tends to yaw the boat to leeward (lee helm). This can be countered by designing the outrigger so that its centre of lateral resistance is 8-15 percent (depending on overall beam) ahead of the centre of lateral resistance of the hull. The keel action of the outrigger then acts along a line forward of the line of action of the centreboard and cancels the above-described lee helm. This is shown schematically in Fig. 2-8. The outriggers should be

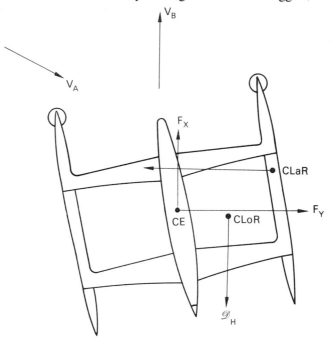

Fig. 2-8. Balance of yawing torques in a trimaran sailing to windward.

mounted in such a way that both are clear of the water with the boat at rest under average load conditions. In this way the trimaran can sail on its central hull alone when running and thereby gain a distinct advantage in resistance over a similar catamaran. For windward work, the high positioning will allow a somewhat greater heel angle. This has the effect of putting the windward outrigger several feet out of the water where its round bottom will not often encounter a wave. When going to windward, the centreline of the hull lies at an angle λ, the leeway angle, to the course line if the keel (centreboard, dagger board, leeboard, etc.) is laterally symmetrical. In this case drag can be reduced by toeing the outriggers out by an angle equal to the leeway angle experienced on a beam reach (Edwin Doran, Jr., AYRS 83 B, 18 (1976).) It is also advantageous to incline the vertical centreline of the outriggers outward at the bottom by an angle of not more than 15°. This has the effect of making the outrigger a smooth extension of the curved cross beams, thus reducing the stresses at that junction. As the boat heels the outrigger is brought into an upright position corresponding to minimum drag.

In order to prevent a rapid rise in outrigger drag with increasing immersion, the DLR of the fully pressed outrigger must be quite low. This means that the reserve volume must be contained in length rather than freeboard. The limitation of such a long needle-like outrigger is the strength-to-weight ratio of its construction. It is likely that the current (1977) practice of making outriggers about 80% as long as the hull is too conservative and that longer outriggers should be contemplated.

Proas are the least understood multihull type. The original Micronesian proa consisted of a lean asymmetric hull to leeward and a heavy log outrigger (counterbalance weight, really) to windward. This craft was sailed by a large and agile crew who arranged themselves to windward as needed to keep the log flying just clear of the water. The few modern adaptations of the proa that have been built in a size suitable for offshore sailing have been 'Atlantic' proas with the hull to windward and a submersible or low-buoyancy outrigger to leeward. The exception to this is Newick's *Cheers*, a schooner-rigged proa that featured equal hulls. *Cheers* was the only one of the lot to have enjoyed any racing success.

The best way to think of a proa in modern terms is to visualise a trimaran with the windward outrigger and cross beams sawn off. The Micronesian outrigger or counterweight becomes our hull and the Micronesian hull becomes our full-buoyancy outrigger. So far as the hull and outrigger shapes are concerned, they should resemble the forward half of the trimaran repeated on both ends.

Comparing the proa with a catamaran in terms of performance, we see that in the daysailing sizes, the concentration of crew weight to windward gives the catamaran all the advantage of the proa. In the larger size where mobile crew weight is not a factor, the proa retains the advantage of permanent weight bias to windward. In comparison with the trimaran, the fact of not having to carry a windward outrigger and cross beams constitutes a big advantage in weight and windage. The weight saved can go into huskier and longer cross beams to put the centre of gravity further to windward. Clearly, in the oceangoing sizes, proas will be faster than either catamarans or trimarans on all courses. Catamarans may be faster than trimarans going to windward owing to a possible windage advantage. Trimarans will usually be faster than catamarans on a run or in light airs to the extent that outrigger drag can be minimized or eliminated. The difference in performance between these two types is much less than the performance advantage of the proa.

On the basis of Eq. (2-21) and the fact that rough water drag is proportional to WF^2, we might suppose that multihulls having a sufficiently low DLR might obey a simplified drag equation such as

$$\frac{R}{W} = aF^2, \tag{2-23}$$

where a is approximately constant. This turns out to be true. In a paper presented at the 1977 Royal Yachting Association Speed Sailing Symposium, Derek Kelsall reported that tank testing of a five-foot trimaran model and resistance calculations for several multihulls using the International Offshore Multihull Rule (IOMR) equations both resulted in smooth parabolic curves of the form of Eq. (2-23) where the constant a varied from boat to boat over a range of 0.025-0.032. Notably, Kelsall sees no hump in the curves owing to wave drag as is seen in monohull data. This is apparently obscured by the rough water drag.

Now let us discuss the question of accommodation arrangement. The minimum requirement is a bunk for each crew member, a galley, head, a few shelves and storage lockers, and a place to sit in comfort for eating, navigating, or what-have-you. The facilities and arrangements required by individuals vary too much for detailed recommendations containing my own biases to be useful. Some general observations on accommodation where performance is the overriding consideration are in order, however.

The waterline beam of the hull must be kept small as we have seen; however the hull can be flared or stepped above the waterline. This allows bunks, lockers, shelves, and so on to be fitted in the narrow hull and still give room for movement without too much elbow friction.

In a catamaran, there will be a strong temptation to build accommodation space on the deck between the hulls, because of the narrowness of the individual hulls. This has the effect of raising the centre of gravity higher off the water and adding windage. As we shall see when we discuss structural problems, there is good reason to have some sort of thick connecting structure which can comprise a cockpit and enclosed space with seated headroom.

In the trimaran and proa, accommodation is restricted to the hull. The proa, needing longitudinal symmetry, will have a centre cockpit. In the trimaran, cockpit location is optional. Other than that, the accommodation space and layout of proa and trimaran may be similar.

Weight must be kept out of the ends of the hull or hulls in order to keep the moment of inertia about the pitching axis low. This will have the effect of limiting the amplitude of pitching motions and ensure that they are rapidly damped. This is vital in reducing rough water drag. Only the central half of the hull should be regarded as habitable. Human nature being what it is, any small spaces that you as a designer do not wish to have heavy stores put into can be filled with plastic foam. This will serve to absorb shock in case of damage, though foam is heavy in large volumes and should not be overdone. Do *not* regard standing headroom as a necessity in small yachts. I would not build a coach house structure at all but would continue a fair line from the beams straight across the hull. In the fore-and-aft direction, the sheer line of the hull should curve smoothly into this raised deck. Flat areas should be avoided everywhere. They are structurally, aerodynamically, and aesthetically unsound. The trimaran *Three Cheers* designed by Dick Newick and shown in Fig. 2-9 is a good example of the type of continuous deck and outrigger beam structure recommended.

To close this chapter on hulls and outriggers, I would like to pass along some thoughts on drawing hull lines. This method is used by a number of naval architects but does not seem to have entered

Fig. 2-9. *Three Cheers* showing the smooth merging of outrigger beam structure with hull.

the text books; I learned it from Newick who revealed it at the World Multihull Symposium in Toronto, Canada, 14-17 June, 1976.

Hull fairness is all important. Hollows or abrupt changes of hull curvature through deviations from fairness constitute sources of eddies and turbulence that can ruin a boat's performance.

One first draws the profile and load waterline onto the station lines (Fig. 2-10a). Next draw the plan view showing the sheer line and keel (Fig. 2-10b). Finally, draw the maximum cross section (Fig. 2-10c). The centreline and sheer intersect points for the cross sections can now be transferred from the profile and plan views to a body plan. The problem is now to draw the remaining cross sections such that the hull will everywhere be fair, without curvature changes or reversals over short distances. For a hull of fairly simple shape such as the proa hull (by Newick) shown here, a template can be constructed that includes the curve of the maximum section with a fair extension on either end. The master template for Newick's proa is shown in Fig. 2-10d). By keeping the x mark on the template along the reference line AA′ and either set of intersect points on the template curve, all cross sections will change proportionally and the lines will be fair. The problem is therefore reduced from one of constructing the sections by experienced eyeball to one of finding one suitable reference line. It will usually be a straight line as is the case here, although it can also be a smooth curve.

25

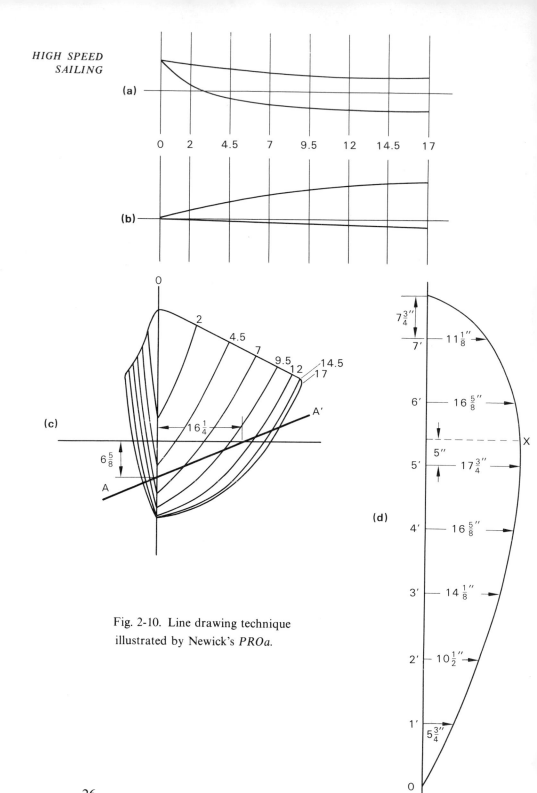

Fig. 2-10. Line drawing technique
illustrated by Newick's *PROa*.

REFERENCES

1 Castles, Walter, *AYRS 83B, 13* (1976) and private communications.

2 Havelock, T. H., *Proc. Roy. Soc. A, 138*, 339 (1932).

3 Hogner, E., *Arkiv fur Matematik, Astronomi, och Fysik, 17*, (1923).

4 Kelsall, Derek and John Shuttleworth, *Multihull International, 111*, 67 (1977).

5 Lunde, J. K., Society of Naval Architects and Marine Engineers (1951).

6 Mason, P. A., *Proceedings of the Sixth AIAA Sailing Symposium, Los Angeles, 1975.*

7 Peters, A. S., *Communications of Pure and Applied Mathematics, 2*, 123 (1949).

8 Weinblum, G. P., *Report 710*, David Taylor Model Basin, Washington, D.C. (1950).

3 STRUCTURAL DESIGN

We have seen that our quest for higher sailing speeds is in large degree a matter of eliminating 'fat'. We cannot afford to make everything excessively robust as one would for a Thames barge. Structural design must be carefully considered in order that stress points can be identified and allowed for without overbuilding.

The strain field of a sloop-rigged monohull craft is indicated in Fig. 3-1 where tensions have been labelled with a T and compression strain by a C. The need for a very stiff forestay in order to provide an appropriate shape for the headsail calls for very stiff hull construction. This conclusion is also valid for multihulls, except that there the situation is more complex. In the case of a trimaran, the mast is stepped in the hull as with a monohull and the longitudinal view Fig. 3-1(a) applies. Very often the shrouds will be taken to the outriggers in order to eliminate the need for diamond stays and crosstrees. In this case the outrigger beams are then subject to considerable bending moment and must be stiff enough to keep mast bending to within close limits. In the catamaran the mast is stepped onto the connecting

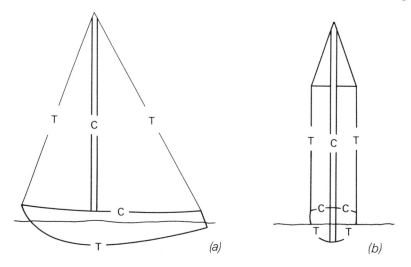

Fig. 3-1. The strain distribution in a monohull sailing boat.

structure between the hulls which must tolerate a concentrated load in addition to the other strains imposed. For this reason, we shall recommend that multihull craft be designed with a sailing rig suited to their structural configuration, that is, a rig that does not require highly stressed shrouds and stays connected to the hull, outriggers, or connecters. The details of this recommendation are given in the following chapter.

By releasing ourselves from the requirement of a bar-taut forestay, our main structural attention may be transferred to the hull/outrigger connecting beams and the strain imposed upon them. In Fig. 3-2 we show a heeled multihull. In this case upward buoyant force on the lee outrigger or hull imposes a bending strain on the beam that has the effect of putting the upper half of the beam in compression and the lower half in tension. If the buoyancy is taken to equal the weight

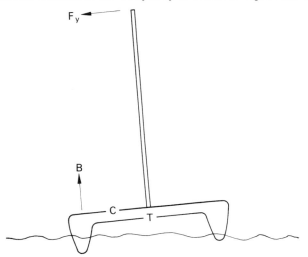

Fig. 3-2. Bending strain in the beam structure of a heeled multihull.

of the boat in the extreme case where the weather hull is just lifted clear of the water, the maximum strain in the beam σ_{max} in pounds per square inch is given by the formula

$$\sigma_{max} = \frac{Wlh}{I}, \tag{3-1}$$

where l is the length of the beam (equal to the centreline to centreline beam of the boat), h is the half-thickness of the beam, and I is a quantity known as the areal moment of inertia that depends on the cross sectional configuration of the beam. For a solid homogeneous rectangular beam of half-thickness h and width a, I is

$$I = \tfrac{2}{3}ah^3, \tag{3-2}$$

and for a similar hollow beam with the same overall cross section dimensions and skin thickness τ (see Fig. 3-3), I is

$$I = \tfrac{2}{3}a[h^3 - (h - \tau)^3]. \tag{3-3}$$ 29

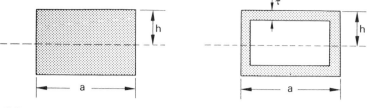

Fig. 3-3.

For a solid beam of circular cross section with radius r, the moment of inertia is

$$I = \frac{\pi}{4} r^4 \tag{3-4}$$

and for the corresponding tube of wall thickness τ

$$I = \frac{\pi}{4} [r^4 - (r - \tau)^4]. \tag{3-5}$$

If the lee hull or outrigger is equipped with a leeway resistor (board or plate), then there will be a compression stress imposed on the beams as shown in Fig. 3-4. If one considers the weight of the boat

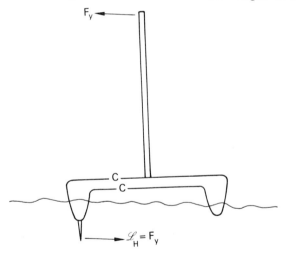

Fig. 3-4. Compressive strain in the beam structure of a multihull sailing to windward.

to be of the order of the maximum value of F_y, then the compression strain is given by

$$\sigma_{max} = \frac{W}{A} \tag{3-6}$$

where A is the cross sectional area of the beam material, that is $A = ha$ for the solid rectangle and $A = 2\tau(h + a)$ for the hollow rectangle.

Finally, we have torsional or shear strain established by the tendency of the hulls to pitch independently in a seaway. This is illustrated

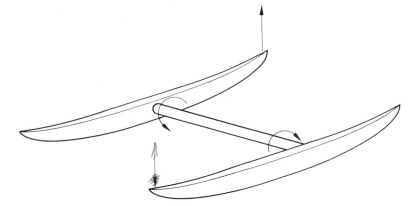

Fig. 3-5. Torsional strains owing to differential pitching.

by Fig. 3-5 which shows two hulls connected by a single cylindrical beam such that one hull is supported by its bow and the other hull by its stern. This situation can arise in ocean sailing and represents wracking strains at their worst. In the case shown, the torque applied to the beam will be approximately $\frac{1}{2}WL$ where W is the weight of the boat and L is its length. This torque will twist the beam through an angle ϕ given by

$$\phi = \frac{WLl}{2GI_P},$$ (3-7)

where G is the shear modulus (pounds per square foot) and I_P is the polar moment of inertia which for a solid circular cylinder is $\frac{1}{2}\pi r^4$. The energy stored in such an elastic deformation given by

$$\mathscr{E} = \frac{W^2L^2G^3}{2I_P l}.$$ (3-8)

This energy is considerable and is extracted from the boat's forward motion. For this reason and others, limber connecting structures should be avoided. By inspecting Eq. (3-8), we see that the only variable over which we have considerable control is I_P, the polar moment of areal inertia. If we contemplate an arrangement of two beams of radius r spaced a distance b apart as shown in Fig. 3-6, then the polar moment of inertia of the two-beam arrangement will be proportional to b^3r

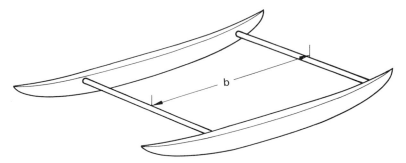

Fig. 3-6. Twin connecting beams.

31

which is much greater than for the single beam. The maximum shearing strain in each beam will be of the order of

$$\sigma_{max} = \frac{4WLr}{\pi b^4} \qquad (3-9)$$

which for a sufficiently large separation distance b presents no problem.

In order to put this analysis into some sort of useful perspective, we will make the feasible assumption that $r \approx 0.1l$, $b \approx l$, $L \approx 2l$. Then the bending, compressional, and torsional strains given by Eqs. (3-1), (3-6), and (3-9) respectively will be in the ratio 4000 : 100 : 0.8. Thus we see that from a strength point of view, if we design to accommodate the bending strains, the compression poses no problem. The even smaller figure for torsional strain is deceptive. True, there is no real danger in wringing the beams off, however very great strains are imposed on the beam points of attachment. Ideally these terminations should be sandwiched solidly between two bulkheads in the hull and outrigger(s).

In racing designs, quite often a truss has been used instead of a beam for outrigger attachment. This arrangement is shown in Fig. 3-7(a).

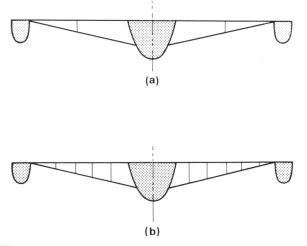

Fig. 3-7. Truss connectors.

Such a truss can carry very high loads for its weight, however the upper member is subject to a compressional load that may be as much as ten or fifteen times the weight of the boat. This member can therefore fail by buckling unless it is braced at frequent intervals to the lower member as shown in Fig. 3-7(b). All told, arched beams of variable cross section terminating in an inclined outrigger provide the best solution to the problem. No more than two beams are necessary; the addition of a third beam between the outer two is inefficient in terms of strength to weight ratio.

Now let us say something about construction materials. For multihulls the choice is effectively limited to cold moulded wood construction, reinforced plastic, or light alloy. In order to evaluate these various materials your attention is directed to Table 3-1 in which a number of materials and composites are listed in order of increasing strength-to-weight ratio starting with mild steel. The first column gives the specific weight relative to water with a value of 1.00. The next two columns give the ultimate tensile and compressive strengths and the last column gives Young's modulus defined as the ratio of the force per unit area to the specific elongation as a measure of stiffness.

Table 3-1. Physical and mechanical properties of boatbuilding materials.

Materials	Specific Weight	Ultimate tensile strength, 10^3 lb/in^2	Ultimate compressional strength, 10^3 lb/in^2	Young's modulus 10^6 lb/in^2
Mild steel	7.8	70	68	29
GRP (chopped strand mat)	1.45	13	20	1.0
African Mahogany	0.50	7	6.7	1.1
Aluminum alloy BS N8 or ASTM 5083	2.7	46	44	10.3
GRP (Woven roving)	1.6	32	14	1.9
GRP (cloth)	1.7	40	30	2.1
'E' glass style 181 in polyester	1.6	45	40	2.5
Kevlar style 281 in epoxy	1.3	75	~12	3.8
Carbon fibers in epoxy	1.5	170	150	17

Wood construction has received a considerable shot in the arm by the development of the epoxy saturation technique largely by the Gougeon Brothers in the US. Complete encapsulating of the wood enables the low moisture content of seasoned veneers used in the layup to be maintained. This has the effect of better than doubling the strength particularly in bending and compression. In addition, the epoxy contributes its own considerable compressional strength. The result is a method of construction that allows very light and strong boats to be built for a modest price in materials (even good woods are relatively cheap). Cold moulding is quite labour intensive however, and is generally not suitable for production. For the one-off builder it is a highly appropriate method and many very good multihulls have been built in this way. Another possible wood construction with great stiffness properties involves sandwich construction. A balsa core can be epoxy glued between thin skins of mahogany to produce a composite construction having a 50 percent weight advantage over solid mahogany in terms of flexural rigidity. This layup would have 33 relatively low impact resistance; however this can be augmented considerably by employing a polypropylene cloth in the outer epoxy layer.

Steel is not a particularly good material for multihulls in the usual yacht sizes although it becomes competitive for boats (ships) of over 100 feet in length. The lower limit for plate thickness is 3/16 inch owing to the fact that welding distorsions become difficult to control for thinner plates and the margin for corrosion vanishes. These objections are not valid for light alloy, however. In addition, the surface can be left completely unpainted as aluminium forms a surface oxide that is quite inert. Care with electrolysis must be taken even to the extent of avoiding mooring to piers with steel piling or, even worse, rafting to a wooden vessel with copper sheathing. Welding must be done under an inert argon atmosphere in order to avoid oxide formation, so this method is hardly suitable for the backyard builder.

Table 3-2. Lay up weights and strengths for reinforced plastic sandwich construction.

Material	oz/ft^2	Ultimate strength of 1 ft wide sample, lbs
CSM in polyester		
3/4 oz.	3	3870
1 oz.	4	5160
1.5 oz.	6	7740
2 oz.	8	10,300
Cloth in polyester		
6 oz.	1.33	4510
8 oz.	1.8	6100
10 oz.	2.25	7620
Woven roving in polyester		
14 oz.	3	8640
16 oz.	3.5	10,100
18 oz.	4	11,500
24 oz.	5.25	15,100
'E' glass in polyester		
style 181	2	8100
Kevlar in epoxy		
style 281	1.2	9570
style 243	1.6	14,300
Carbon fibres in epoxy	2	32,600
Airex 01/18		
1/4 in	2	
3/8 in	2.75	
1/2 in	3.75	
5/8 in	4.5	
3/4 in	5.5	
Airex 01/30		
5/8 in	8	
3/4 in	10	

With the advent of exotic reinforcement materials such as Kevlar and carbon fibres, plastic construction and more particularly sandwich construction using PVC foam offers the ultimate in light weight, high strength, and stiffness. Moreover this method requires less skill than wood construction and is quite feasible for the backyard builder. As an aid to design, Table 3-2 gives the weight in oz/ft^2 of various reinforced plastic composites and Airex PVC core material. In the second column is given the ultimate tensile strength of a one foot wide sample layer. From this we can see that adequate tensile strength can be had even with very thin skins. The main reason for using thick skins is to provide for the aging properties of the plastic. Polyester and epoxy both deteriorate under solar ultraviolet radiation by forming hairline cracks and checks that slowly spread into the lay-up. The author has seen hulls produced for off-shore powerboat racers with extremely thin layups. These hulls take a terrific pounding and are usually obsolete after a year or so—long life is sacrificed. Construction of multihull sailing craft may also be approached in this way if long life is not needed. Do not scrimp in high stress areas, however.

Reinforced plastic/sandwich construction can also be used on such heavily stressed members as boards and rudders. In this case it is a very good idea to use a heavy chopped strand mat to form shear webs between the two skins as shown in Fig. 3-8. The surface lay-up of

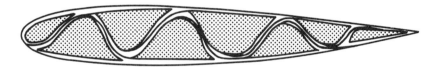

Fig. 3-8. GRP/sandwich rudder construction.

such structures should employ carbon fibres and glass mat in alternating layers to build up the necessary compressional strength. For this application the heavy (01/30) grade of Airex should be used as a core material. Where the board bears against another structural member as occurs, for example where a dagger board protrudes from its trunk, the skin and shear webs should be somewhat thicker in order to tolerate the severe local compressive strains.

One may also contemplate building masts and other spars using epoxy with exotic reinforcement materials. Dick Newick has produced a 36 foot mast for a proa in this way. This mast has a 6 inch diameter at the deck and tapers to 2.44 inches at the head. Each half was layed up in a tapered form of PVC pipe using alternating layers of 281 Kevlar, 243 Kevlar, and Fortaeil CG-5 graphite fibre in epoxy. An overlapping tab is included in each half so that the two halves can be snapped together and fastened with self-tapping screws. This mast, which weighed 55 pounds before hardware was added, failed at the bottom of the sail track carrying 204 sq ft of sail to windward on a very stiff proa in a 20 knot wind. Newick blames the kevlar for the compression failure and intends to use all carbon fibre in epoxy for his next exotic mast.

REFERENCES

1 Buhler, Vance, *Fiberglass Sandwich Standard Details*. Bequia, St. Vincent, W. I., 1976.

2 Cannell, D. and J. Leather, *Modern Developments in Yacht Design*. New York: Dodd, Mead, and Co., 1976. Chapter 7.

3 Gougeon, Jan, Joe, and Meade, *West System*. Gougeon Brothers, Inc., 1973.

4 Gougeon, Jan, Joe, and Meade, *Graphite Fibers*. Gougeon Brothers, Inc., 1975.

5 Johannsen, T. J., *One-off Airex Fibre glass Sandwich Construction*. Buffalo, N.Y.: Chemacryl, Inc., 1973.

6 Mahinske, E. B., *AYRS, 85A*, 28 (1976).

7 Miner, L. H., et al, *Kevlar 49 Aramid, A New Material for Boat Hull Construction*. Second SNAME Chesapeake Sailing Yacht Symposium. 1975.

8 Scott, R. J., *Fiberglass Boat Design and Construction*. Tuckahoe, N.Y.: John de Graff, Inc., 1973.

9 Verney, Michael, *Complete Amateur Boat Building*. London: John Murray, 1959.

10 Warring, R. H., *The New Glass Fibre Book*, Hemel Hempstead, Herts.: Model & Allied Publications Ltd. 1971.

11 Wynn, Peter, *Foam Sandwich Boatbuilding*. Camden, Maine: International Marine Publishing Co., 1972.

12 Various authors, *AYRS, 85B*, 1976.

4 SAILS AND LATERAL STABILITY

The force F_A generated by the sails is given by the expression

$$F_A = \tfrac{1}{2}\rho_A V_A^2 A_S C_A \qquad (4\text{-}1)$$

where ρ_A is the mass density of air at sea level under standard conditions ($\rho_A = 2.38 \cdot 10^{-3}$ slug/ft^3), V_A is the apparent wind speed, A_S is the sail area, and C_A is a numerical coefficient. As we saw in Chapt. 1, this force can be decomposed into a lift force $\mathscr{L}_A$

$$\mathscr{L}_A = \tfrac{1}{2}\rho_A V_A^2 A_S C_L, \qquad (4\text{-}2)$$

and a drag force

$$\mathscr{D}_A = \tfrac{1}{2}\rho_A V_A^2 A_S C_D, \qquad (4\text{-}3)$$

such that

$$F_A = \sqrt{\mathscr{L}_A^2 + \mathscr{D}_A^2}. \qquad (4\text{-}4)$$

The lift coefficient C_L is known to be an approximately linear function of the angle of attack α up to the point of stall, and to depend in addition on the aspect ratio A of the sail defined as

$$A = \frac{S^2}{A_S}. \qquad (4\text{-}5)$$

In this equation, S is the *span* of the sail which is equal to its height if air is free to flow across the foot of the sail from one side to the other as is normally the case. If the foot of the sail is very near the deck or if it is fenced by an end plate, then the aspect ratio may approach twice its unfenced value. Thus, for example, if a triangular sail has a height one and a half times its foot measurement, the aspect ratio would be 3 unfenced and up to 6 fenced, depending on the efficiency of the fence. It is also possible to increase the apparent aspect ratio by fencing the head of the sail, however this usually poses problems in the practical case. In terms of A and α_T, the angle of incidence measured from the angle of zero lift (in degrees), C_L is given approximately by

$$C_L \approx 0.11\alpha_T \frac{A}{A+2}. \qquad (4\text{-}6)$$

Aerodynamic drag is a much more complicated problem. In addition to the drag of the sail, there is also the parasitic drag of the hull, crew, mast, etc. For this reason the practical course of action is to measure the drag by using models in a wind tunnel. One may also obtain these figures by measuring the force on a tethered full size boat using a spring scale. This method is described by Bruce and Morss in their book.

It should be noted that soft sails differ from rigid aerofoils in that they depend critically on a smooth flow on both sides in order to fill them out to the shape the sailmaker built into them. All sails are effectively thin cambered plates or overlapping combinations of such plates and the work that has been done on aerofoil sections for aircraft is largely inapplicable to soft sails.

The camber of a sail is described in terms of the ratio δ/C as shown in Fig. 4-1. A completely flat sail is very inefficient owing to

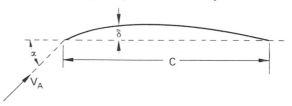

Fig. 4-1. Sail camber.

the fact that flow on the lee side will separate from the sail at the luff. As the camber is increased, the magnitude of F_A increases for any given value of angle of attack. The drag increases faster than the lift so that for any given wind speed V_A and angle of attack α, there is an optimum value of camber. For a beam reach in light airs with an angle of attack of about 30 deg., a camber of 10-15 percent would be best. For the very fast boats of interest to us, a larger proportion of our sailing will be hard to windward in fairly high apparent winds. For this case an angle of attack of about 10-13 deg. and a camber of 3-5 percent are more appropriate. The location of the point of maximum camber should not be too near the luff in order to avoid eddies induced by a too abrupt change in curvature. Experiments by Bowden and others have shown that for headsails the maximum camber should be about 35 percent of the chord behind the luff; for a mainsail the location should be a further 10 percent of the chord aft.

Sailcloth weight is quoted differently in Britain and America. In Britain cloth weight is given as ounces per square yard whereas Americans specify the ounce weight of a yard run for a standard width of 28.5 inches; hence the British ounce specification runs higher than the American by 26 percent for the same cloth. For Terylene/Dacron fabric the recommended weights as a function of sail size and wind strength are given in Fig. 4-2. For sails to be used in high winds on very stiff (in the sense of non-heeling) craft, triple stitching should definitely be specified.

Almost all sail plans in use on sailing craft today are fore and aft rigs with multiple sails. The sail area is broken up into several sails arranged on one or more masts for the reasons that: 1) there is an upper limiting size of 400-600 square feet in a single sail in order that

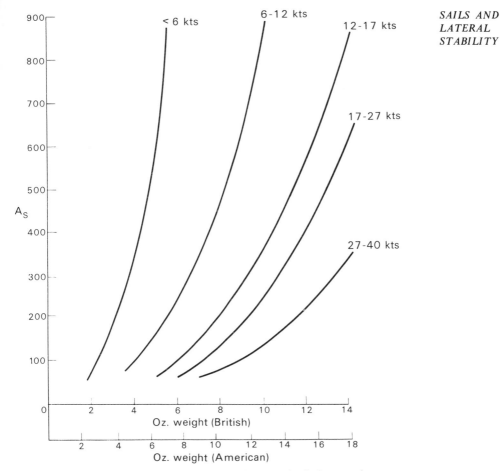

Fig. 4-2. Sailcloth weight as a function of size and wind strength.

one man be able to handle it, 2) the slot effect between the various sails feeds smooth high-speed air to the lee sides of the aft sails in the array thus increasing the force F_A over that generated by a single sail of equivalent area, and 3) sail area can be reduced in steps without upsetting the balance of the boat. The first assumption is certainly valid unless one goes in for electric winching machinery. This will certainly be a valid approach in possible future commercial sailing ships in order to operate with small crews, however for a high speed multihull yacht, the weight of such machinery could not be tolerated. For a sizeable oceangoing craft to be operated single or short handed, the ability to be able to reduce sail in several stages without causing the centre of effort through which the forces act to move about must also be considered an important virtue.

A multicomponent aerofoil such as a cutter rig exerts higher forces for a given incident wind strength, however the drag increases faster than the lift as the number of sails is increased. Thus, from the point of view of minimizing the drag angle, concentration of the sail area into a single sail is more efficient. This fact together with the require- 39 ments for a practical limit to size of a single sail and balanced reefing suggest that we look into what we shall term multiplane rigs wherein sails are set side by side instead of in a fore and aft line. Such an arrangement is shown in the photograph of *Clifton Flasher* in Fig. 4-3. Before we pursue the advantages of this arrangement,

Fig. 4-3. *Clifton Flasher.*

let us dispose of the question of whether or not to use rigid or semi-rigid wingsails such as those used on *Clifton Flasher*.

In general, higher $\mathscr{L}/\mathscr{D}$ and F_A can be obtained in a rigid unarig as compared with a soft unarig and for this reason many of the C-Class catamarans are using them. The penalty paid on such craft for the added power per unit sail area is a weight increase aloft and a correspondingly higher moment of inertia about the heeling and pitching axes. The victory of the American C-Class catamaran *Aquarius V* over her Australian challenger *Miss Nylex* in the 1976 Little America's Cup provides a very practical guide to our choice. *Aquarius* with its soft unarig weighed 470 pounds as opposed to *Miss Nylex* at 650 pounds with her rigid wingsail. This weight advantage proved more significant than the ability of *Miss Nylex* to maintain a lower value of δ_A in strong winds owing to her rigid wingsail. For ocean sailing craft, any rig that cannot be completely reefed or furled should, of course, never be considered.

In the light of these arguments, the optimum multiplane rig would seem to be the pyramid rig shown in Fig. 4-4. This rig consists of two triangular soft sails tilting together at the top with a gap between them equal to the chord at all heights. Each sail can have a relatively high aspect ratio without the centre of effort of the sail plan as a whole being nearly as high as that of a conventional fore-and-aft rig of comparable area. It is found experimentally that the centre of effort located at approximately $\frac{1}{3}$ the height of a triangular sail moves as a

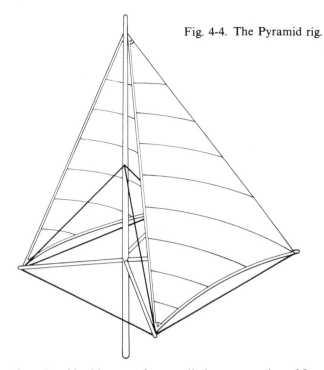

Fig. 4-4. The Pyramid rig.

function of angle of incidence α from a little greater than 35 percent of the chord aft of the luff for small α to 50 percent for $\alpha = 90$ degrees. Thus, by locating 35 percent of the sail area forward of the mast, the rig can always weather-cock when the sheets are released, however the centre of effort is always so close to the vertical pivot axis (the mast) that multifold sheet purchases and winches are rarely required even for fairly large sail areas and high winds.

One of the principal advantages of the pyramid rig so far as multi-hull craft are concerned is that the rig is tuned as regards stay tensions before being placed in the boat. Thus the hull and crossbeam structure need not tolerate the stresses imposed by conventional rigs with their high forestay tension and mast compression, both of which must be borne by the hull. The pyramid rig is stepped upon a thrust bearing of the type shown in Fig. 4-5(a); just below the four gooseneck

Fig. 4-5. Thrust foot bearing and collar bearing for rotating mast.

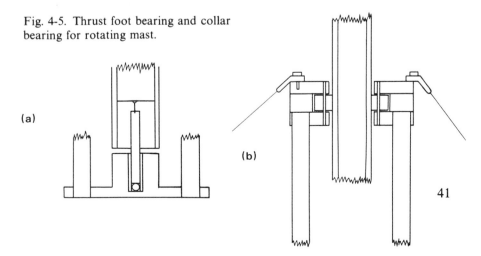

(a)

(b)

fittings a collar bearing featuring teflon rollers as shown in Fig. 4-5(b) is fitted. A masthead thrust bearing might also be used with stays to the extreme corners of the boat if the aspect ratio is high enough, however the rig can be cantilevered from the collar and lower thrust bearings.

Many designers of fast sailing craft have favoured wingsails, full battens with large roach, and other techniques concerned with extending the power available from a *limited* sail area. Without any such artificial limitation, I feel that it is sounder approach to look for the maximum forward driving force for a given tolerable heeling moment with the simultaneous requirement of balanced reefing and minimum weight—maximum simplicity. This approach leads to the pyramid rig.

In order to evaluate the sail carrying ability of a boat in a given wind, we must first find the static stability of the hull array. Figure 4-6(a) shows a catamaran at zero heel angle with F_y and $\mathscr{L}_H$ both

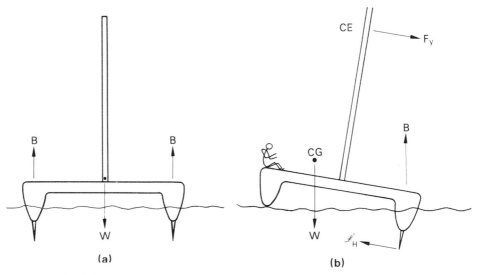

(a)   (b)

Fig. 4-6.

equal to zero. For $F_y = \mathscr{L}_H > 0$, the craft takes on a heel angle θ that reduces the buoyancy of the windward hull to zero at a heel angle $\theta = 10\text{-}12$ degrees. The forces acting upon the hull array in this condition of maximum static stability are shown in Fig. 4-6(b). The righting moment of the hull without the keel and sail forces is approximately given by

$$N_{\text{hull}} = W(\bar{y} \cos \theta - \bar{z} \sin \theta) - bB_0(1 - \theta/\theta_0) \qquad (4\text{-}7)$$

where W is the total weight, $\bar{y}$ is the horizontal distance from the heeling axis in the lee hull to the centre of gravity (half the centreline to centreline beam b in a large cat), $\bar{z}$ is the vertical height to the CG, B_0 is the unheeled buoyancy of the weather hull ($W/2$ not counting crew shift) and θ_0 is the heel angle for which the weather hull lifts out.

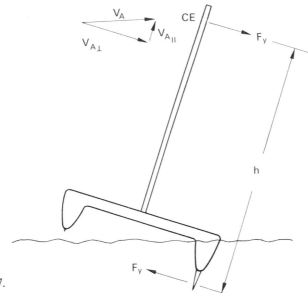

Fig. 4-7.

When a sail is heeled at an angle θ as shown in Fig. 4-7, the driving and transverse forces F_x and F_y decrease with increasing heel angle as $\cos^2 \theta$ to a first approximation. The heeling moment owing to the couple caused by the sail and keel is therefore

$$N_{sail/keel} = hF_y = hF_{y_0} \cos^2 \theta \qquad (4\text{-}8)$$

where

$$F_{y_0} = \tfrac{1}{2}\rho_a V_A^2 A_S C_y \qquad (4\text{-}9)$$

As a realistic numerical example, let us consider a boat having the following parameters: $W = 2500$ lb., $\bar{y} = 10$ ft, $\bar{z} = 2$ ft, $b = 20$ ft, $B_0 = 1250$ lb., $\theta_0 = 12$ degrees. The equation for the hull righting moment then becomes

$$N_{hull} = 25000 \cos \theta - 5000 \sin \theta - 25000(1 - \theta/12) \quad (4\text{-}10)$$

where the last term is zero for all $\theta > 12$. For the sailplan we shall consider a 500 ft^2 conventional rig (sloop, ketch, schooner, etc.) with overall aspect ratio of 3 (unfenced) and a vertical distance $h = 19.9$ ft between the line of action of the keel and sail; 7 feet of this is distance from the foot of the sail to the keel centre of lateral resistance and the remaining 12.9 feet is one third of the height of the specified sail. Thus the sail/keel heeling moment is

$$N_{sail/keel} = 33.8V_A^2 \cos^2 \theta, \qquad (4\text{-}11)$$

where V_A is to be expressed in knots and the coefficient $C_y \approx 1$. The net righting moment as a function of θ and V_A is then found by subtracting Eq. (4-11) from Eq. (4-10). This is plotted in Fig. 4-8. This figure shows us why a catamaran can fly its weather hull in a rather stable fashion at heel angles of 40 or 50 degrees owing to the fact that the stability curves flatten out at the higher wind strengths, reaching a second stability maximum at $\theta = 50\text{-}60$ degrees. If we con-   43

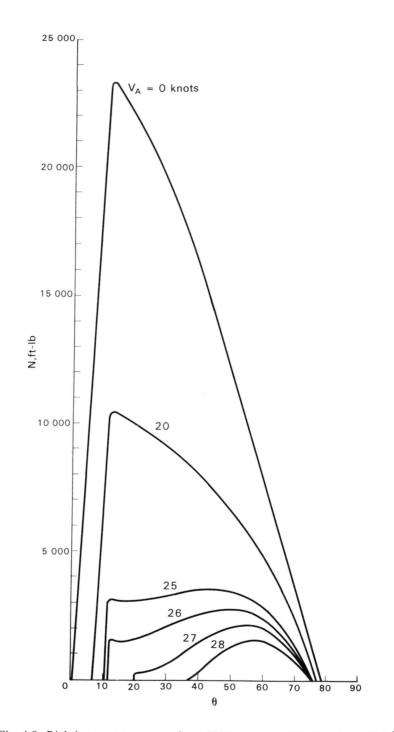

Fig. 4-8. Righting moment curves for a 2500 pound multihull with a 500 ft² conventional rig.

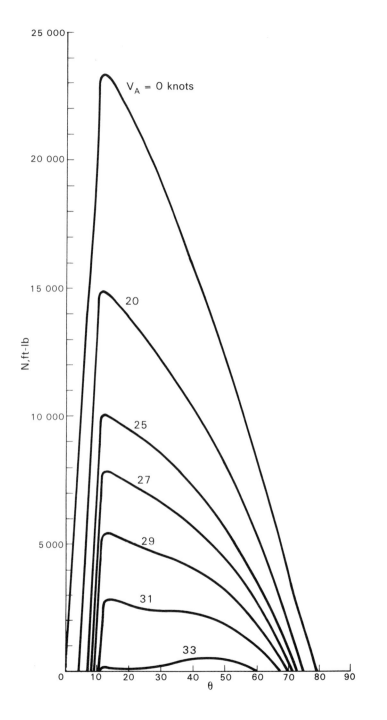

Fig. 4-9. Righting moment curves for the same hull as Fig. 4-8 but with a
pyramid rig having equal drive at $\theta = 0$.

45

sider the maximum operating angle of heel to be that for which the weather hull just starts to lift out, we see that this is reached for $V_A = 26$ knots in the present example.

We now wish to compare the stability of the same hull equipped with a pyramid rig. For this purpose we shall take the two pyramid sails each to have aspect ratio 3 as in the conventional case. The slope angle of these sails will then be about 19.5°. In order to compensate the drive lost owing to the slope angle, we shall make the total sail area equal to $500/\cos^2(19.5°) = 563$ ft^2. The height h in this case, with the same 7 feet from sail foot to keel, is 16.1 feet. The heeling moment of a pyramid rig of slope angle ψ and total area A_S is given by

$$N_{\text{sail/keel}} = F_{y_0}[\cos^2(\theta + \psi) + \cos^2(\theta - \psi)]\left[h \cos \psi - \frac{d}{2} \sin \psi\right] \quad (4\text{-}12)$$

where

$$F_{y_0} = \tfrac{1}{2}\rho_a V_A{}^2 \frac{A_S}{2} C_y \quad (4\text{-}13)$$

and d is the separation distance of the sails at the height of the centre of effort, d equals 2/3 the length of the foot. For our present example, Eq. (4-12) becomes

$$N_{\text{sail/keel}} = 12.5 V_A{}^2[\cos^2(\theta + 19.5) + \cos^2(\theta - 19.5)] \quad (4\text{-}14)$$

As before, the net righting moment as a function of θ and V_A is found by subtracting Eq. (4-14) from Eq. (4-10). The result is plotted in Fig. 4-9. Comparing this plot with that of Fig. 4-8, we see that the pyramid rig sails at smaller heel angles in a given wind and is capable of standing up to higher winds and hence exerting larger driving force than a comparable conventional rig. In the present case the pyramid rigged craft can sail at its maximum operating heel angle of 12 degrees at $V_A = 32$ knots as opposed to 26 knots for the conventional rig and is therefore capable of delivering about 43 percent more driving force. We also see from Figs. 4-8 and 4-9 that one cannot fly the windward hull in a pyramid rigged craft with the ease and relative security possible with a conventional sloop rig owing to the fact that the secondary peak in the righting moment curve is not pronounced for the pyramid. On the other hand, gusts can be parried very quickly with the pyramid rig owing to its direct and single sheet.

In a conventional rig, proper and close control of sail twist is a problem. A kicking strap or vang is helpful but unless the clew can be downhauled by using a semicircular traveller track, uncontrollable twist will occur and rob the boat of about 10-15 percent of its driving force. In the pyramid rig, all three corners of the sail are attached to dimensionally stable points and twist can be controlled quite accurately.

On a dead run, it is very hard to beat a square rigger. The fore and aft rigged vessel tries to imitate the square rigger by hanging all of its sails at right angles to the wind. The pyramid rig, being capable of rotating 360°, can be positioned at the most advantageous angle of attack as determined by the knotmeter. In this way both sails can

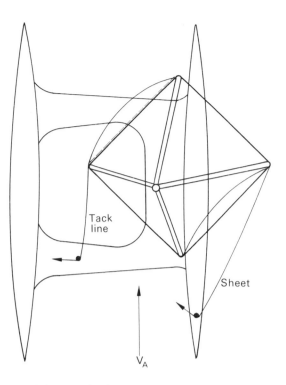

Tack
line

Sheet

V_A

Fig. 4-10. Pyramid rig on a dead run.

drive and the forward sail is not shadowed by the after one. This is shown in Fig. 4-10.

Proas must, of course, have sail rigs that can be reversed end for end when the craft shunts. It was in going over the possibilities in this area that the pyramid rig first came to my attention. In practice, a pyramid rig can be swung around using tack lines quite quickly in order to obtain reverse drive. This amounts to having a remarkably good set of brakes and is an important safety feature in close manoeuvring under sail.

We have seen that from the point of view of hydrodynamic resistance, large boats are better than small ones. This is also true from the standpoint of lateral stability. The righting moment goes as the weight (which scales as L^3) times a distance and therefore scales as L^4 whereas the aerodynamic heeling moment being proportional to A_S times h scales as L^3. Thus large boats can carry proportionally larger sail area for a given V_A and the effect is to increase the speed potential in approximate proportion to $\sqrt{L}$.

In conclusion, the best all around rig for fast sailing would appear to be a pyramid rig with unbattened sails having a geometrical aspect ratio of about three. It is well worth while to fence the foot of the sail. Marchaj has shown that the reduction in induced drag results in a 15-20 percent increase in driving force F_x over an unfenced sail. The additional parasitic drag associated with the four boom struts is more than offset by the greater lift-producing sail area so far as overall drag angle δ_A is concerned.

47

REFERENCES

1 Barkla, Hugh, *AYRS*, *17*, 34 (1958).

2 Bowden, C. E., *AYRS*, *76*, 10 (1971).

3 Bruce, Edmund, *AYRS*, *40*, 23 (1962); *AYRS*, *82* (1976).

4 Doran, Edwin, *Multihull*, *3*, no. 3 (1977).

5 Manners-Spencer, J., *AYRS Airs*, *8*, 28 (1974).

6 Marchaj, C. A., *Sailing Theory and Practice*, New York: Dodd, Mead, & Co. (1964).

7 Various members of AYRS: *AYRS*, *14*, 27 (1957); *AYRS*, *87*, 22 (1977).

5 LATERAL PLANE AND RUDDERS

In order to enjoy a condition of stationary equilibrium, the under-water parts of a sailing boat arrange themselves at an angle λ, known as the leeway angle, to the vector $\mathbf{V}_B$ such that the keel and hull generate a hydrodynamic force $\mathbf{F}_H$ equal and opposite to the aero-dynamic force $\mathbf{F}_A$. In this chapter we shall be concerned to find the means whereby this hydrodynamic force can be generated so as to keep the hydrodynamic drag angle δ_H at a minimum.

In Fig. 5-1 we show the underwater portion of a hull together with

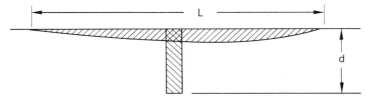

Fig. 5-1.

a rectangular keel. In order to calculate the hydrodynamic lift of this configuration together with the induced drag, we shall treat the keel and hull separately. Following Castles, we write for the lift coefficient

$$C_L = \begin{cases} \left(\dfrac{2\pi A}{A + 2} + \lambda \right)\lambda; & A > 2 \\[3mm] \left(\dfrac{\pi A}{2} + \lambda \right)\lambda; & A \leq 2 \end{cases} \tag{5-1}$$

where λ is in radians and the aspect ratio A is defined by

$$A = \frac{2d^2}{A_K} \tag{5-2}$$

for the keel where A_K is the keel area measured to the waterline. For the hull a similar relation holds where A_P, the vertical projected area of the hull is used in place of A_K and half the span is just equal to the hull draught H. For semi-circular hull sections, $H = B/2$ and $A_P = A_W/\pi$ where A_W is the total wetted area given by Eq. (2-20). 49

Thus the hull aspect ratio is given by

$$A = \frac{4(B/2)^2 \pi}{0.74 \pi L B} = 1.35 \frac{B}{L} \qquad (5\text{-}3)$$

which ranges from 0.04 to 0.12 for hulls of interest to us.

The drag induced by lift production is specified by the coefficient

$$C_{Di} = \begin{cases} \left| \left(\dfrac{4\pi A}{(A+2)^2} + \lambda \left(1 - \dfrac{\lambda}{2\pi} \right) \right) \right| \lambda^2 ; & A > 2 \\[4mm] \left| \left[\dfrac{\pi A}{4} + \lambda \left(1 - \dfrac{\lambda}{2\pi} \right) \right] \right| \lambda^2 ; & A \leq 2 \end{cases} \qquad (5\text{-}4)$$

The total hydrodynamic resistance is then found by calculating the running resistance using the Havelock-Castles equation from Chapt. 2 and adding the induced resistance of the hull and keel

$$R_i = \tfrac{1}{2} \rho_H V_B^2 (A_P C_{Di,\,P} + A_K C_{Di,\,K}) \qquad (5\text{-}5)$$

for a leeway angle λ. By comparing the total resistance $\mathscr{D}_H$ to the total lift $\mathscr{L}_H$ given by

$$\mathscr{L}_H = \tfrac{1}{2} \rho_H V_B^2 (A_P C_{L,\,P} + A_K C_{L,\,K}) \qquad (5\text{-}6)$$

for a variety of leeway angles, it can be shown that the lift-to-drag ratio is a maximum and hence δ_H is a minimum for $\lambda = 4\text{-}5$ degrees.

Next we consider the question of how big to make the keel. This can be decided by calculating the underwater lift and setting it equal to the side force F_y generated by the sail

$$F_y = \tfrac{1}{2} \rho_a V_A^2 A_S C_y, \qquad (5\text{-}7)$$

where

$$C_y = C_L \cos \beta + C_D \sin \beta. \qquad (5\text{-}8)$$

Thus we must know $\beta(V_T, \gamma)$ and hence V_B/V_T before we can find the keel area and vice versa. Since we only need to know the maximum keel area and, for a low DLR hull, the hull lift can be neglected, thus the data given in Fig. 5-2 for the Newick Val-class trimaran *Galliard* is useful. For windward sailing, $C_A \approx C_y$, thus we see that $C_y \approx 1$ over a fairly broad range of windward courses.

Setting Eq. (5-6) with $C_{L,\,P} = 0$ equal to Eq. (5-7), with $C_y = 1$ we find

$$\frac{A_K}{A_S} = \frac{\rho_A C_y}{\rho_H C_{L,\,K}} \left(\frac{V_A}{V_B} \right)^2, \qquad (5\text{-}9)$$

or

$$\frac{A_K}{A_S} = 3.42 \cdot 10^{-3} \left| \frac{\sin \gamma}{\sin(\gamma - \beta)} \right|^2, \qquad (5\text{-}10)$$

where the coefficient $C_{L,\,K}$ has been taken to equal 0.35 appropriate to an aspect ratio of 6 and $\lambda = 4$ degrees. The term in square brackets results from the evaluation of $(V_A/V_B)^2$ via the application of the law of sines to the sailing triangle (Fig. 1-1). The measured values of β

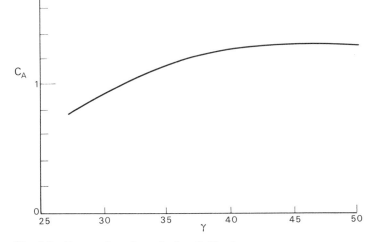

Fig. 5-2. C_A as a function of γ for *Galliard*

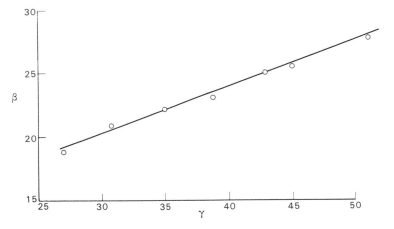

Fig. 5-3. β as a function of γ for *Galliard*.

versus γ for *Galliard* are given in Fig. 5-3. Using this data, Eq. (5-10) is plotted in Fig. 5-4. On the basis of this curve I would select a maximum keel area of $0.015A_S$ as being about right. As a general requirement, we must be able to vary the keel area. Thus we are left with the choice between centreboards, daggerboards, and leeboards.

A centreboard has the advantage of being able to fold back into its slot if the boat runs over an obstacle or is grounded. For a high aspect centreboard this calls for a long trunk slot which has the strong disadvantage of being a source of considerable eddy resistance. In addition, the force generated by the centreboard applies a strong torque to twist the trunk which must consequently be of massive construction.

In a daggerboard arrangement the slot is minimal since the board only moves vertically, however there is no protection against impact 51

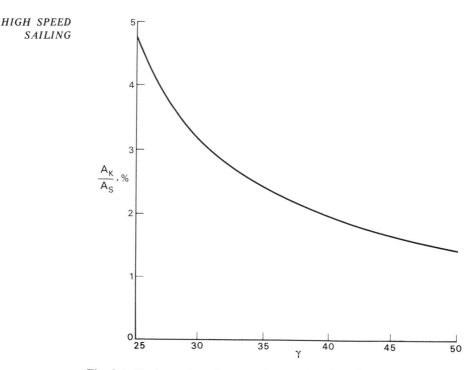

Fig. 5-4. Keel area to sail area ratio as a function of γ.

or grounding. Dick Newick favours daggerboards in his designs and has incorporated a foam filled "crash box" behind the board to minimize damage from impact. Both centreboards and daggerboards, when mounted in the hull rather than the outrigger(s) constitute a considerable invasion of the accommodation space.

What about leeboards? These are seen to offer several advantages. They are quite suitable for shallow water sailing since not only can the operating depth of the board be varied but, by arranging to be able to vary the longitudinal position of the pivot point, the centre of lateral resistance can be maintained in line with the centre of effort of the sails to retain the balance on all courses. In water deep enough to accommodate only the hull, leeboards can still provide sufficient lateral lift for windward sailing. In calculations involving lift coefficients under such conditions, the aspect ratio A must be replaced by $A' = A \cos \phi$ where ϕ is the sweep angle. Leeboards operate on the outside of the hull and do not require a trunk with its attendant structural problems and intrusion into accommodation. All parts are therefore readily accessible for maintenance or repair. No problems from stones jamming the boards—as happens with daggerboards and centreboards—are experienced.

The disadvantages of leeboards are relatively minor. First, there is the necessity of dropping one and raising the other when coming about. If the trimaran or catamaran is equipped with a self-tending pyramid rig, the job of leeboard changing should not be excessively demanding. Since the leeboard is essentially a surface-piercing vertical hydrofoil,

there exists the possibility of air ventilation down the low pressure
side (more detail on this phenomenon in Chapter Six), however this
can be handled either by fencing just below the waterline or by operating
the board at a slight forward sweep angle as suggested by David
Keiper. One wonders why leeboards have not been used more often
on racing multihulls and I can only conclude that leeboards must
arouse visions of Thames barges in most designer's minds and have
therefore not been considered in proper context.

Another interesting possibility in the design of a leeboard system
is to have the pivot mounts not only movable fore and aft but also
capable of rotation about a vertical axis over a range of a few degrees.
In this way the leeboard can be set to an angle of attack
independently of the hull in order to reduce or eliminate the hull leeway
angle and thereby also eliminate the induced drag of the hull. The
leeboards may also have asymmetric sections thereby reducing their
induced drag for the same lift production.

Now let us consider rudders. The function of a rudder is, of course,
that of applying a yawing moment to change the course of a boat.
The rudder types that can be applied to high-speed sailing craft are the
over-the-stern or transom mounted type, the rudder behind a skeg, and
the spade rudder as shown in Fig. 5-5. In evaluating the hydrodynamic

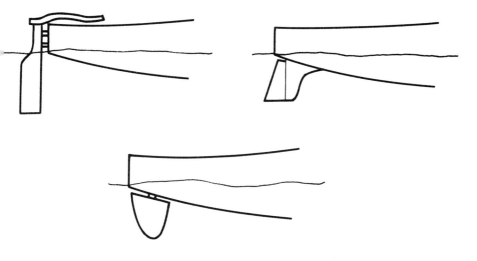

Fig. 5-5. Three types of rudders appropriate to fast sailing craft.

properties of a rudder we are not so much interested in optimum
$\mathcal{L}/\mathcal{D}$ as has been our concern with other aero- and hydrofoils.
Rather we want a maximum side force capability when the rudder is
deflected and a minimum friction drag when the rudder is symmetrically
aligned and is producing no lift. The maximum rudder area A_R
required for efficient low speed manoeuvrability depends on the configuration and aspect ratio, however a good average figure is

$$A_R \approx 0.07(A_P + A_K) \tag{5-11}$$

Rudder design entails many compromises. In order to place the

rudder in a smooth flow and avoid entrainment of surface air, the
rudder should be fairly deep, but not so deep as to promote heeling.
The choice of aspect ratio is likewise not so simple. High aspect ratios
as we know, give rise to larger forces per unit area for a given angle
of attack than low aspect ratios do. The angle of attack for which
flow separation occurs (stall angle) is smaller for a high aspect rudder
than for one of a lower aspect ratio, however. There is, therefore,
an optimum value of aspect ratio in order to maximize the side force
per unit area. It is found that an aspect ratio of 1 is about right for
a spade rudder. For a rudder-skeg combination the aspect ratio
(including the skeg) should be 0.5-1. In a transom-mounted rudder
the upper 1/3 or so is ineffective owing to the turbulence of the wake,
hence an overall aspect ratio between 1 and 2 is best for this type.

In choosing a section shape for a rudder we note that a flat plate
or any section with a sharp leading edge stalls at a relatively low
angle of attack regardless of aspect ratio. Consequently we require a
symmetrical section with an elliptical leading edge. The maximum
thickness should occur about 1/3 of the chord from the leading edge
and should amount to about 12 percent of the chord. In most cases
the rudder should be unbalanced, that is, its pivot axis should be
slightly forward of the centre of effort of the rudder at all rudder angles.
Since tests have established that the centre of effort moves from about
20-25 percent of the chord aft of the leading edge at low angle to about
40 percent at large angle, the rudder shaft should be located in the
forward 20 percent of the rudder. Multihulls can be blown backward
quite rapidly at times, hence the unbalance must be minimal in order
that the strength of the rudder not be exceeded under these conditions.

For catamarans the practice will normally be to fit a rudder at the
stern of each hull. In this case the area equation (5-11) must be applied
to each hull separately. In a trimaran, a single rudder will be fitted
to the hull. For the high speeds encountered by the boats in which
we are interested, the rudder must be very strong. The skeg type
of rudder has a decided structural advantage since the rudder has
bearings at the bottom as well as the top whereas both the spade and
stern-hung rudders are cantilevered. One possibility with obvious
advantages is to build the rudder-skeg into a daggerboard arrangement
as shown in Fig. 5-6. The daggerboard will tear through the rear of the
trunk if struck and the damage will be trivial. Lanyard attachment to

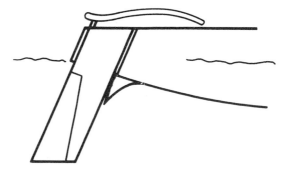

54   Fig. 5-6. A daggerboard skeg rudder.

the transom permits recovery of the unit. The daggerboard as a whole
may easily be withdrawn from the trunk for maintainance or repair
as necessary or to reduce resistance in an otherwise self-steering boat.

Proas pose a special problem in rudder design since they must sail equally well in either direction. Both ends must be fitted with a rudder which must either be retractable or must work in concert with the one on the other end. Newick's 1968 proa *Cheers* used the former approach with a combination rudder and daggerboard in either end of the windward hull. The rudder was located in the middle part of the board so that it only operated with the board fully down. The forward board was lowered partially to balance the boat. This scheme is shown in Fig. 5-7. In his 1974 *PROa*, Newick used non-retractable spade

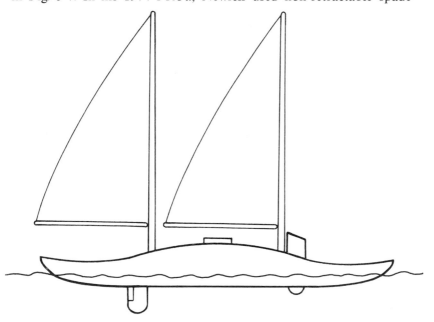

Fig. 5-7. Daggerboard rudder system in *Cheers*.

rudders at either end of the leeward hull. These rudders work together to push the bow in one direction and the stern in the other. In the *Cheers* system both boards must be adjusted for height and the connecting rod to the whipstaff must be fastened to one tiller and unfastened from the other. This is acceptable if one shunts only seldom, however it is too much work for general sailing. The 1974 *PROa* system is much simpler, but both systems are vulnerable to grounding damage.

We have examined some possible lateral resistance and rudder systems. Before we can make a proper choice we must examine the factors influencing yaw stability, that is, the inherent ability of a boat to be able to steer itself.

In monohulls, heeling is the dominant factor in self-steering ability. If a perturbation causes a monohull to fall off from a close hauled course, then the side force and heel angle will increase. This has the effect of moving the line of action of the sailforce F_A further 55 to leeward of the line of action of the keel F_H, thereby establishing a torque to cause the craft to head up or luff. Likewise a luffing perturbation is countered by a reduction of heel angle and a consequent torque tending to bear away. On a broad reach the heeling effect which still dominates monohulls is a destabilizing one. For example, a perturbation that causes the yacht to fall off will now decrease the heel angles and therefore cause the tendency to fall off to increase. Consequently, monohulls can usually (but not always) be induced to steer themselves to windward, but they are generally very poor at inherent self-steering with the wind abaft the beam.

For multihulls, the conditions influencing self-steering ability are more subtle. First consider effects associated with the sails. In Fig. 5-8 we show a catamaran with a low aspect unarig yawing in the

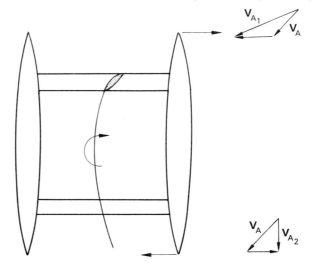

Fig. 5-8.

clockwise sense. The yawing motion induces a sideward component of velocity which adds to V_A to produce the wind velocity vectors V_{A1} and V_{A2} as shown. The effect is an increased angle of attack at the luff and a decreased angle of attack at the leach. This shifts the pressure distribution toward the luff and induces a correcting torque in the counter clockwise direction. This effect is obviously stronger for low aspect or divided rigs than for high aspect sloops or cutters. Secondly, we note that a luffing perturbation, if slow enough, will lead to a reduced angle of attack overall. Thus the rate dependent correction will not be excited. However, as we know, the location of the centre of effort moves forward as the angle of attack decreases and this provides a correcting torque which is angle rather than rate dependent. Here again, low aspect ratio increases the effect. If the rig is a divided one, then marginal yaw stability can be augmented by sheeting the mizzen freer than the main and headsails. If a falling off perturbation occurs, the mizzen will increase its drive to a greater degree than the other sails and hence seek to push the bow back to windward. In a luffing perturbation, the mizzen looses its drive first and the boat will therefore seek to bear away.

For the keel a similar situation with respect to rate dependent correction holds as with the sails. This explains why long keel workboats of fifty years ago self-steer so nicely while a modern 12-metre boat is a helmsman's nightmare. A single low aspect keel is of course, inappropriate because of the large wetted surface area. The solution is to have at least two high aspect keels separated by a considerable longitudinal distance as shown in Fig. 5-9. The main keel can be

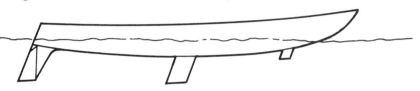

Fig. 5-9.

located near the axis of rotation and the aft keel can be a high aspect stern-hung rudder as is common with dinghies. This configuration can be balanced and steered by a vane gear or sheet-to-tiller gear, however its hands-off-the-tiller steering capabilities (the best ones to have) will be poor. A skeg-rudder combination as the after keel for a sufficiently large skeg area to rudder area ratio will work quite well however. A small trimming board in the bow adds flexibility.

This rate dependent keel effect is augmented by an angle dependent effect. When close hauled, a bearing-away perturbation causes the speed of the boat to increase. Since the side force changes relatively slowly with angle, the increase in V_B must be compensated by a decrease in the leeway angle λ. The centre of effort of the keel moves forward as λ decreases thus inducing a correcting torque to weather. On a broad reach the effect is a destabilizing one since falling off slows the boat. In practice, with twin high aspect keels the angle-dependent keel effect is negligible either as a stabilizing or destabilizing influence. The effect of a freer sheeted mizzen in the sails is duplicated underwater by balancing with a slight weather helm. The rudder then either gains or looses lift faster than the keel to provide a correcting torque.

There is some argument in trimarans for placing the leeboards in the outriggers rather than close on either side of the central hull. When running under heavy conditions a broach is always to be guarded against. If both leeboards are down and are toed in by 4 degrees or so, then any broaching action will cause the leeward board to gain lift as the other board looses it. The additional moment arm gained by locating the boards in the outriggers magnifies this stabilizing effect proportionally. The result is altogether analogous to the effect of asymmetric catamaran hulls as discussed in Chapt. 2.

To sum up, catamarans and trimarans might well use a skeg rudder arrangement as shown in Fig. 5-6 in their hull or hulls with leeboards forward. The leeboards may be mounted in cases that are capable of swinging aft if struck. Leeboard depth is varied by running the board up or down in the trunk thus the mount can be fixed and need not be movable longitudinally. This type of leeboard arrangement is shown in Fig. 5-10.

The best steering, leeway resisting, and yaw stabilizing system for a

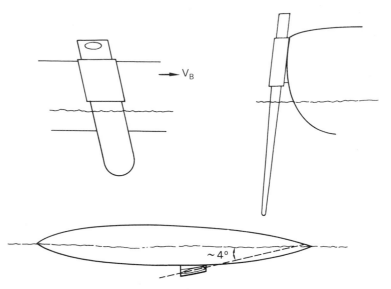

Fig. 5-10. A cased leeboard system.

proa is probably twin steerable leeboards near either end of the out-rigger (leeward hull). The system would be very like that shown in Fig. 5-10 except that the cases will be mounted with zero leeway angle and the bottom of the leeboards will consist of a spade rudder. The two rudders will work together driven by a wheel amidships as shown in Fig. 5-11. As the major job of the shunting operation the rudders are turned around 180 degrees to put them in a balanced position and the bow board is raised somewhat with respect to the aft board. This can be done with tackle or, on a large proa, with hydraulics.

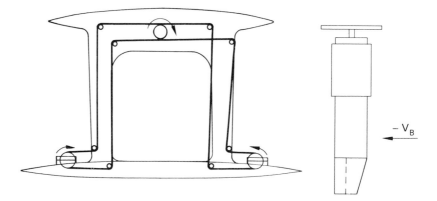

Fig. 5-11. A proa steering system.

REFERENCES

1 Castles, Walter, AYRS, *83B*, 13 (1976).

2 Follett, Tom; Dick Newick, and Jim Morris, *Project Cheers*, London: Adlard Coles, Ltd. 1969.

3 Herbert, Tom et al, *Self-Steering*, AYRS, *13*, (3rd ed.) (1974).

4 Letcher, J. S., *Self-Steering for Sailing Craft*. Camden, Maine: International Marine Publishing Co. (1974).

5 McMullen, Michael, *Multihull Seamanship*. New York: David McKay Co., Inc. 1976.

6 Marchaj, C. A., *Sailing Theory and Practice*. New York: Dodd, Mead & Co. (1964).

7 Morwood, John, AYRS, *89*, 15 (1977).

8 Norwood, J., AYRS, *84A*, 4 (1976).

9 Olsen, K. J., *Rudder Design for Sailing Craft*, AYRS, *79*.

10 Rands, M. B., AYRS, *73*, 60 (1970).

11 Thomson, J. H., AYRS, *84B*, 6 (1976).

6 HYDROFOIL APPLICATIONS

The tendency to view hydrofoils only as a means to lift the hull or hulls clear of the sea is conditioned by the fact that hydrofoils have been applied mainly to engine-powered craft which are subject to a less complex set of forces than sailing craft. In Fig. 6-1, to obtain a quantitative feeling for the problem, we have plotted the vertical lift-to-drag ratio (weight-to-resistance) of a typical multihull craft as a function of $V_B/\sqrt{L}$ using Eq. (1-8). Also shown is a curve labelled hydrofoils, which is characteristic of a set of deeply immersed hydrofoils together with the necessary struts. From this figure we see that the buoyancy/resistance figure for a good hull is greater than the lift/drag value of hydrofoils up to a value of $V_B/\sqrt{L} \approx 2.5$. The attainment of such high speeds requires that the boat be able to counter a large heeling moment and still keep the sail as near vertical as possible. It is in this regard that the primary application of hydrofoils to sailing craft arises. Although foil stabilization was used in the outrigger craft of Madagascar and Dar es Salaam, Edmond Bruce was the first to formulate the physics correctly.

In Fig. 6-2 we show a multihull craft equipped with a canted hydrofoil to leeward. In the (a) part of this figure the craft is at rest and the only forces in effect are the weight W which is opposed by the buoyancy B operating along the same vertical line. In the (b) part of the figure, the boat is in motion at a constant speed and a state of dynamic equilibrium exists. The basis for leaving the buoyancy in the same vertical line as the weight in this case is the assumption that we will be successful in eliminating the heeling moment. Were this assumption not justified, then the centre of buoyancy would move to leeward as the boat heels.

In order to enjoy a state of equilibrium, an extended body must experience no net forces in the vertical or horizontal directions. Also, the moment of the forces (torque) about any point must vanish. For the present purpose we can neglect the forces normal to the page, that is, the driving force and the drag. The vanishing of the forces implies

$$B = W - \mathcal{F} \cos \theta, \tag{6-1}$$

and

$$F_y = \mathcal{F} \sin \theta. \tag{6-2}$$

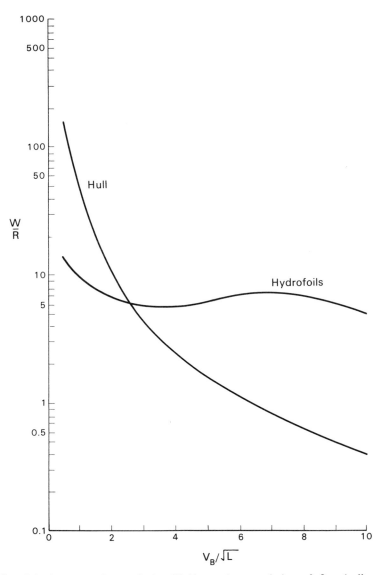

Fig. 6-1. A comparison of the lift/drag characteristics of fine hulls and hydrofoils.

Multiplying Eq. (6-1) by sin θ and Eq. (6-2) by cos θ (where θ is the dihedral angle of the foil) and adding, we find

$$B \sin \theta + F_y \cos \theta = W \sin \theta,$$

or

$$F_y = (W - B)\tan \theta. \qquad (6\text{-}3)$$

By virtue of Eq. (6-2), we see that the vertical component of the hydrofoil force is

$$\mathscr{F} \cos \theta = F_y \operatorname{ctn} \theta. \qquad (6\text{-}4)$$

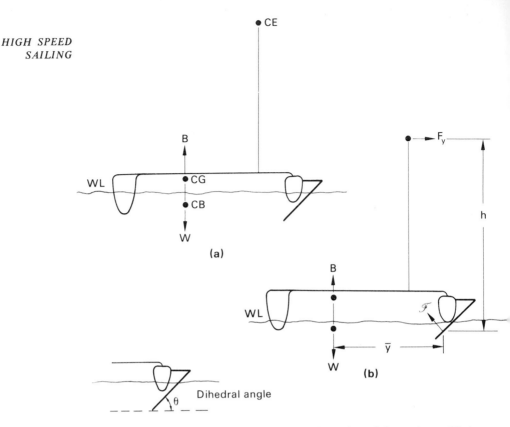

Fig. 6-2. A Bruce foil-equipped sailing craft in static and dynamic equilibrium.

Using Eq. (6-3), we can now express the buoyancy as

$$B = W - F_y \operatorname{ctn} \theta. \tag{6-5}$$

Thus our hydrofoil sailing craft in dynamic equilibrium can be reduced to the force diagram shown in Fig. 6-3. By taking moments about any point on this figure and setting them equal to zero, we are led to the following key relation:

$$F_y(h - \bar{y} \operatorname{ctn} \theta) = 0. \tag{6-6}$$

Since F_y is never zero except in the trivial static case, the quantity in parentheses must vanish in order to ensure the vanishing of the heeling torque. Thus

$$\bar{y} = h \tan \theta. \tag{6-7}$$

Having found the dimensional relationship that causes the heeling torque to vanish, we must now ask ourselves the following question. How large can F_y be (or, equivalently, how much sail can be carried in a given wind) in order that Eq. (6-6) still be satisfied? The answer to this question is contained in Eq. (6-5). This equation describes the decrease of B, the buoyancy, as F_y increases, thus increasing the vertical component of the foil force. As F_y approaches a value $W \tan \theta$, the buoyancy approaches zero as the hulls lift out. At the point of liftoff,

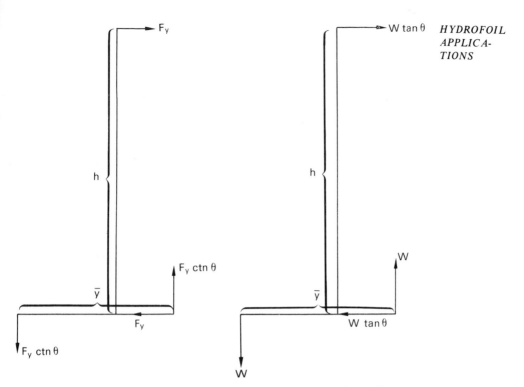

Fig. 6-3. Equivalent force diagram for sub-lift-off speeds.

Fig. 6-4. Equivalent force diagram at lift-off.

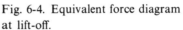

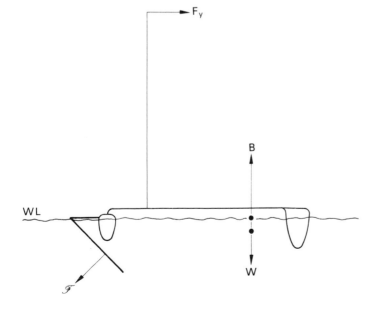

Fig. 6-5. A Bruce foil craft with windward stabilization.

the force diagram tends to that shown in Fig. 6-4. The force components F_y ctn θ of the righting couple have reached a maximum value W; the corresponding righting moment is therefore

$$N_{\max} = W\bar{y}, \tag{6-8}$$

and any further increase in F_y over the value $W \tan \theta$ will lead to capsize. If we were to replace the foil unit by a light nonsubmersible hull, the same value of maximum righting moment obtains. The virtue of the leeward canted foil arrangement, known as a *Bruce foil*, is that 1) no heeling at all is experienced up to the point of liftoff, thus keeping the driving effort of the sails at a maximum, and 2) the heeling force F_H has been converted into vertical lift thereby reducing the drag of the hulls.

It is also possible to cancel the heeling torque by using a canted foil to windward that depresses rather than lifts the boat as shown in Fig. 6-5. One may also derive Eq. (6-6) for this case. There are two outstanding disadvantages to this arrangement, however. First, the hulls are being depressed and so the hull drag is a rapidly increasing function of F_y. Second, and even more important, the windward foil arrangement is *unstable*. If a leeward foil pops out of the water owing to wave action, then the heeling torque acts to quickly reimmerse the foil. If a windward foil comes unstuck, the heeling torque is then uncountered by a windward depression and the craft will probably capsize very quickly. For this reason, a leeward Bruce foil or foils having a dihedral angle θ such that $\bar{y} = h \tan \theta$, is the best choice for vertical lift and lateral roll stabilization. In choosing the dihedral angle θ, we find that angles in the range 40-45 degs are probably best. If the angle is very much greater than 45 degs, then the beam necessary to satisfy Eq. (6-7) becomes excessive. If θ is too small, the foil area or leeway angle must be large in order to generate a horizontal force component equal to F_y.

Now let us see what type of hydrofoils are suitable for use on sailing craft. Hydrofoils can be separated into two classes depending on whether the blades are wholly immersed by struts or whether the foils themselves pierce the surface. In order for the boat to have vertical stability, the hydrofoils must somehow manage to "see" the air-water interface and thus be able to respond to a vertical displacement perturbation in such a way as to rapidly restore the original flight altitude. Fully immersed foils can only do this by operating very near the surface where lift is a sensitive function of depth, or by having a surface sensor that transmits orders to the hydrodoil for required changes in angle of attack. The first method, employed extensively by the Russians in their large powered river craft, is useless in any sort of sea. The second method has been explored by Hook and others. At the present stage of development, this feedback method is, in the author's estimation, too heavy and complicated to be appealing.

The outlook for surface-piercing hydrofoils is much better. To a first approximation, the lift exerted by a hydrofoil at a given speed varies linearly with its depth of immersion and with the angle of attack of the water flow onto the foil α. In Fig. 6-6a we see a hydrofoil experiencing a flow with angle of attack α. If a downward displacement

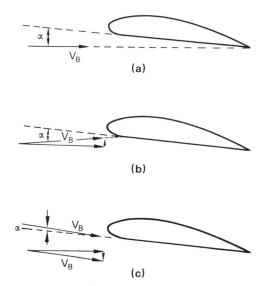

Fig. 6-6. Changes in angle of attack induced by vertical motion.

occurs, the hydrofoil experiences an additional component of fluid velocity from below. This is interpreted as an increase in the angle of attack as shown in Fig. 6-6b. If the displacement is upward, the effect is a reduction of α and the foil tends to loose lift in opposition to the perturbation (Fig. 6-6c.) The effect is entirely analogous to that described in Chapter 5 for yawing sails and keels. Thus we see that the hydrofoil resists vertical displacements with a force proportional *both* to the displacement and the rate of displacement. This tendency to resist changes in the vertical direction is powerfully augmented in the case of surface-piercing foils by the automatic variation of the foil area; that is, if a perturbation depresses the foil below its equilibrium water-line, the action of the increased area tends to restore the equilibrium while the change of apparent angle of attack tends to damp the motion and prevent overshoot.

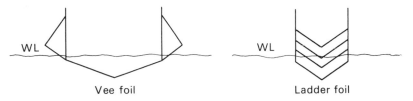

Fig. 6-7. Monoplanar and multiplanar surface-piercing hydrofoils.

Surface-piercing hydrofoils may be mono- or multi-planar as shown in Fig. 6-7. For smooth-water sailing the monoplanar foil works quite well, however for offshore sailing the ladder foil should be preferred. The large reserve of unimmersed foil in the ladder arrangement can exert high lift as the foil enters a wave. The monoplanar foil is generally used in powered vessels designed to operate foil-borne only over a narrow range of speeds. In sailing, our source of power and   65 consequent speed varies over a wide range. In a multiplanar ladder, the foil section can be varied from a high lift, low $\mathscr{L}/\mathscr{D}$ section near the static waterline to a section more appropriate to high speeds at the bottom of the ladder.

Now let us examine the effect of wave action upon hydrofoils. In Fig. 6-8 we have indicated the motions of individual elements of water

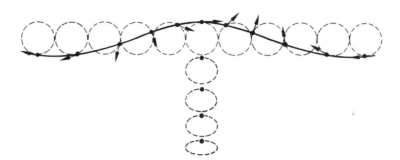

Fig. 6-8. Water particle motion under wave action.

as a wave passes through from left to right. These orbits are circular with a diameter equal to the wave height at the surface and tend to a shuffling back and forth at greater depth. Now consider a hydrofoil-borne craft sailing to weather, that is, moving against the wave motion. Since the water on the front of the wave is rising, the foil sees this as an increase in angle of attack and the lift is increased. The hydrofoil therefore tends to climb the wave rather than hold a constant altitude. On the back side of the wave, the water is falling. This is seen as a decrease in angle of attack, lift decreases, and the boat tends to contour the back side of the wave as well. In a following sea, the situation is more serious. If a foil-borne craft moves to leeward fast enough to overtake the waves, then it will tend to plow into the back side as the apparent angle of attack of the foil decreases. It is for just this situation that the ladder foil arrangement realizes its maximum advantage.

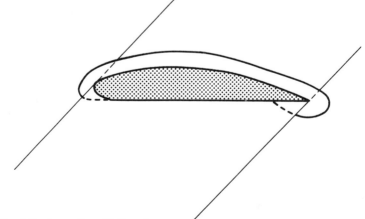

66   Fig. 6-9. An antiventilation fence.

The pressure on the curved surface of a hydrofoil is lower than that on the flat side. In surface-piercing operation, a portion of the curved surface of the hydrofoil near the air-water surface may experience a pressure below atmospheric. This leads to the formation of a cavity and the entry of air from the surface, thus resulting in a loss of lift. This phenomenon is known as *ventilation*. It is controlled by the use of fences as shown in Fig. 6-9. It is also helpful if the foil or strut can be angled forward in order that the surface water encountering the member is given a velocity up the strut. This technique was used by Keiper on the trans-Pacific foil trimaran *Williwaw* with considerable success.

At higher speeds for a given chord length, the pressure at some point on the hydrofoil finally falls below the vapour pressure of the surrounding water. Bubbles then form as local boiling commences. These bubbles move aft along the foil surface and as the pressure rises, the bubbles collapse. The impulsive pressures on the foil surface as these cavitation bubbles collapse are several thousand pounds per square inch and pitting of the foil surface usually results. The speed at which cavitation begins lies in the 40 knots plus range for most hydrofoils and so does not concern us other than for a large sailing speed record machine. Such an ultimate sailing craft might well be equipped with a ladder foil arrangement having a supercavitating foil as its bottom rung. Such a section is shown in Fig. 6-10.

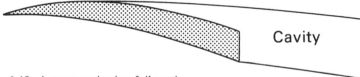

Cavity

Fig. 6-10. A supercavitating foil section.

We would now like to address ourselves to the question of the configuration into which the hydrofoils should be arranged on a sailing boat. It is immediately evident that the hydrofoil array must have considerable extent in both the transverse and longitudinal directions, hence the buoyancy for sub-foiling conditions must be provided by an arrangement of multiple hulls, that is, a catamaran, trimaran, or proa.

The hydrofoil configuration will be symmetrical about the longitudinal centreline when applied to a symmetrical hull layout such as the catamaran or trimaran. The two simplest configurations in such a case are the *aeroplane* and *canard*. These two configurations are shown in Figs. 6-11 and 6-12. The aeroplane configuration features the Bruce foils in a forward location, carrying most of the weight, and the steerable stern foil serves as a pitch stabilizer. The canard configuration has its lightly loaded pitch stabilizer in the bow and the Bruce foils near the stern. The question of which hull arrangement is best with which foil arrangement may have to be decided by the question of accommodation or crew placement, however, for off-shore work a trimaran-canard is likely to be best.

Fig. 6-11. Philip Hansford's *Mayfly*, an aeroplane-catamaran.

Fig. 6-12. Donald Nigg's *Flying Fish*, a canard-trimaran.

As we have previously noted, a hydrofoil unit is analogous to a damped spring by virtue of the dependence of its lift on the depth of immersion and rate of immersion. The stiffness of the spring is proportional to the rate of change of lift with depth of immersion (small chord = stiff foil) and the damping rate is proportional to the rate of change of lift with angle of attack since vertical velocity of the unit results in a proportional change in angle of attack. A foil of large chord operated at a low angle of attack has such a high damping rate. If the bow and stern foils have identical characteristics or if the stern foil is stiffer, a pitching perturbation can induce a porpoising type of instability. In conditions where one is running into a following sea, a highly damped stern foil and a stiff bow foil provide excellent

Fig. 6-13. George Chapman's *Tiger*, a Bruce foil proa.

pitch control. In practical terms, this calls for a lightly loaded bow foil operated at a high angle of attack and a stern foil carrying about 85 percent of the weight operated at the angle of attack corresponding to maximum $\mathscr{L}/\mathscr{D}$. In a hull-borne craft, these characteristics are obtained by using a fine bow with generous flare above the waterline and a broad, flat run off at the stern. Thus the canard configuration should be expected to be far superior to the aeroplane configuration in pitch control. In lateral roll control there is not much to choose between the two. If the two main foils are both canted lifters (the leeward Bruce foil configuration) then the angle of leeway will tend to increase the angle of attack of the lee foil and decrease the angle of attack of the weather foil. In order to operate on either tack in satisfaction of Eq. (6-7), the beam would have to be approximately twice the height of the centre of effort which is unlikely. Thus a laterally symmetrical hydrofoil craft will experience some heeling to leeward which also serves to nullify the lift of the windward foil by lifting it partially or wholly out of the water.

Now let us examine the laterally asymmetric proa foil configuration. This arrangement has a decided advantage in heeling control since, using a sail plan of modest overall aspect ratio such as the pyramid rig, the condition for heeling cancelation can be met. In order to gain pitch control, it is necessary to split the Bruce foil into two units located at either end of a long, slim leeward hull as shown in Fig. 6-13. The bow unit can then be operated at a slightly higher angle of attack than the stern unit in order to provide the necessary longitudinal distribution of stiffness and damping.

At this point I would like to address the question of extending the righting moment of an ideal Bruce foil proa beyond the value given by Eq. (6-8). It is obvious that this can only be done by adding weight to the windward hull or by using a windward hydrofoil unit that exerts a downward force. Both of these suggestions have advantages and disadvantages.

69

Harry Stover has suggested that a water scoop might be used to increase the weight of the windward hull as boat speed and heeling moment increase. The main problems with this suggestion would seem to be the large drag induced by such a scoop and the inability to regain buoyancy in the windward hull on short notice. The windward depressing foil also must pay the penalty of increased drag owing to the fact that the Bruce foils have not only to lift the weight of the boat, but also the windward foil force K. For this case, assuming the foil units to operate at a lift/drag ratio of 10, it can be shown that the effective horizontal lift/drag ratio in terms of which the drag angle δ_H is defined is

$$\left(\frac{\mathscr{L}_H}{\mathscr{D}_H}\right)_{\text{eff}} = \frac{10\left(1 + \dfrac{K\bar{y}}{Wh}\operatorname{ctn}\theta\right)}{\csc\theta\left(1 + \dfrac{K\bar{y}'}{Wh}\operatorname{ctn}\theta\right) + \dfrac{K}{W}\operatorname{ctn}\theta} \tag{6-9}$$

where K is the windward depressing force

$$K = F_y\operatorname{ctn}\theta - W, \tag{6-10}$$

and $\bar{y}'$ is its lateral distance from the centre of effort of the Bruce foils. In the limit of large K/W, Eq. (6-9) approaches

$$\lim_{K/W\to\infty}\left(\frac{\mathscr{L}_H}{\mathscr{D}_H}\right)_{\text{eff}} = \frac{10\bar{y}'/h}{\csc\theta(\bar{y}'/h) + 1}, \tag{6-11}$$

which represents a bounded increase in the drag angle δ_H. Thus the attainable value of V_B/V_T decreases, however given enough wind, the sail-carrying power is so increased that the actual top speed is higher than before. Such righting moment enhancement by either the water scoop or hydrofoil technique should be contemplated for a speed record machine sailing in protected waters, however for offshore work, it seems wise to stick to the simple twin Bruce foil arrangement.

Various amateurs have built and sailed hydrofoil boats, however with a few notable exceptions these boats have not shown a clear performance advantage over hull-borne craft. Partly this has been due to overweight and inappropriate configurations. For the most part, I am convinced that the main problem has been overestimation of the lift owing to the use of oversimplified theory. The analogy with aerodynamics is not perfect; the proximity of the air/water interface introduces corrections that *must* be taken into account.

The hydrofoil lift force $\mathscr{L}$ is given by

$$\mathscr{L} = \tfrac{1}{2}\rho_H V_B^2 A_F C_L, \tag{6-12}$$

where C_L is the lift coefficient. As we have seen, C_L increases linearly with angle of attack α over its normal operating range, that is, up to the stall point. The slope of this curve can be shown to be 2π where α is measured in radians or $\pi^2/90 \approx 0.11$ where α is measured in degrees for a foil of infinite length acting in an unbounded medium. Thus

$$C_{L_0} = 2\pi\alpha_T \tag{6-13}$$

where α_T is the angle of attack as measured from the attitude of zero lift. This ideal lift coefficient slope is reduced by various factors.

In a bounded fluid, the low pressure on the upper surface of the foil not only lifts the foil, but also distorts the free surface above it such as to reduce the pressure differential and consequently decrease the lift. The perturbation of the water surface manifests itself as a transverse wave. This effect can be taken into account by including two correction terms. The loss of lift due to pressure relief is similar in nature to the drag induced on the lower wing of a biplane by the upper wing. It can be approximated by multiplying the ideal slope 2π by a factor

$$\kappa = \frac{(4h/c)^2 + 1}{(4h/c)^2 + 2}, \tag{6-14}$$

where h is the depth of submergence of the hydrofoil and c is its chord. The lift loss is only about 5 percent for $h/c = 1$, (this also applies to the pyramid rig). The loss increases to 50 percent for $h/c = 0$, at which point the foil becomes a planing surface having an ideal lift slope of π for infinite span. The wave loss can be accounted for by adding a term

$$\Omega = \frac{\exp(-h/cF^2)}{2F^2}, \tag{6-15}$$

where F is the Froude number defined on the basis of the chord

$$F = \frac{V_B}{\sqrt{gc}}. \tag{6-16}$$

This function is plotted in Fig. 6-14 for several values of h/c. It can be shown that the peaks of these curves occur at a boat speed $V_B = \sqrt{2gh}$ that is well below take-off speed. Thus hydrofoils pass through the wave 'hump' with ease at low speed which is, of course, one of their chief virtues. It should be mentioned that this approximation breaks down when the craft is operated in shallow water. The maximum speed of a gravity wave in water of depth d is $\sqrt{gd}$. For boat speeds exceeding $\sqrt{gd}$, the wave train cannot keep up and a more complex theory must be used.

Just as in aerofoil theory, a hydrofoil of finite span is subject to a further lift loss and induced drag as a result of the vortex system at the tip or tips. A wing of aspect ratio A and elliptical spanwise loading has an induced lift angle and drag given by

$$\frac{\alpha_i}{C_L} = \frac{C_{Di}}{C_L^2} = \frac{1 + \sigma}{\pi A}, \tag{6-17}$$

where $\sigma = 0$ for aerofoils and

$$\sigma = \frac{A}{A + 12h/c} \tag{6-18}$$

for hydrofoils. The equivalence of induced drag and its associated induced lift angle is depicted in Fig. 6-15. Physically, this loss is associated with diverging lateral waves arising from the trailing vortices.

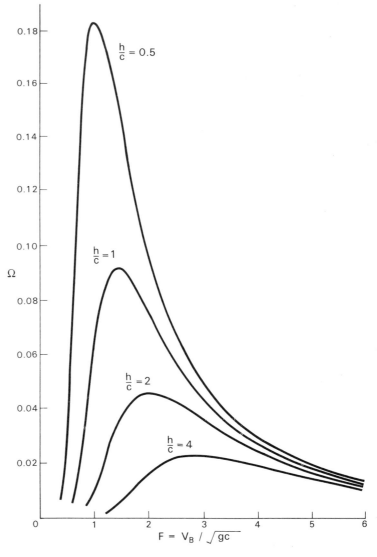

Fig. 6-14. Free surface wave function as a function of Froude number and depth of immersion.

This correction applies only for high Froude numbers; two-dimensional theory gives a reasonable estimate at low speeds.

For modest aspect ratios, deviation from the assumed elliptical planform can be taken into account by multiplying the ideal slope 2π by a correction factor

$$E = (1 + 2/A^2)^{-1}. \tag{6-19}$$

The flow velocity that generates lift is perpendicular to the span. Thus, if foils with a sweep angle ϕ are used, then the two-dimensional lift slope must be multiplied by $\cos \phi$. This same sort of correction is necessary for dihedral. The angle of attack is defined in the vertical

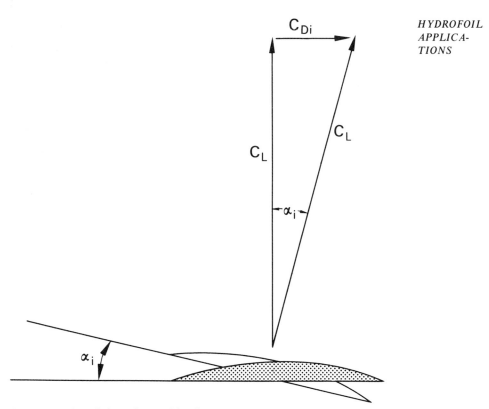

Fig. 6-15. Induced drag due to lift effects.

plane and is therefore decreased by a factor cos θ where θ is the dihedral angle.

The definition of aspect ratio for hydrofoils is a bit more involved than for aerofoils owing to the presence of struts and, in the case of surface-piercing foils, the air-water interface, both of which inhibit spanwise flow. In Fig. 6-16a we show a horizontal hydrofoil of span b supported by two struts separated by a distance a. The effective aspect ratio for this configuration has been shown to be well approximated by

$$A = \frac{b}{c}\left[1 + \left(\frac{a}{b}\right)^3 \frac{h}{b}\right]. \tag{6-20}$$

For a T-foil having a single strut, $a \to 0$ and $A = b/c$ as expected. For a V-foil as shown in Fig. 6-16b, Eq. (6-20) can be applied to the equivalent configuration shown with dashed lines and one finds

$$A = \frac{b}{c}\left(1 + \frac{h}{b}\right) = \frac{h}{c}(1 + 4 \operatorname{ctn} \theta). \tag{6-21}$$

The effective aspect ratios for the asymmetric dihedral foils shown in Figs. 6-16c and d are similarly evaluated.

Collecting the contributions from Eqs. (6-13)-(6-15), (6-17), and (6-19), the lift coefficient can be estimated as

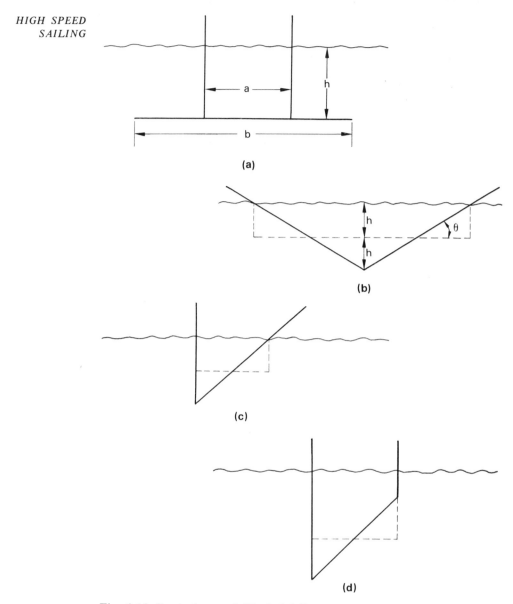

Fig. 6-16. Equivalence of dihedral foils to a horizontal foil vertical strut combination.

$$\frac{\alpha_T}{C_L} = \frac{1 + 2/A^2}{2\pi\kappa \cos \phi \cos \theta} + \Omega + \frac{1 + \sigma}{\pi A}. \tag{6-22}$$

Only for large Froude number, high aspect ratio, and deep submergence does this equation reduce to the simple expression

$$C_L = 2\pi\alpha_T\left(\frac{A}{A + 2}\right), \tag{6-23}$$

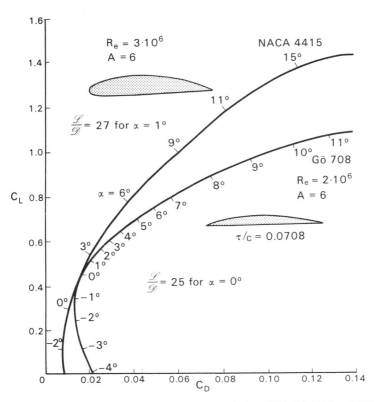

Fig. 6-17. Comparison of the section characteristics of NACA 4415 and Gö 708.

often used by amateur experimenters.

The drag coefficient for the lifting part of the hydrofoil unit (excluding struts) is given by

$$C_D = C_{D_0} + C_L{}^2\left(\Omega + \frac{1 + \sigma}{\pi A}\right), \qquad (6\text{-}24)$$

where C_{D_0} is the section drag coefficient. In the absence of experimental data, C_{D_0} may be estimated using the empirical formula:

$$C_{D_0} \approx 0.004(1 + 1.2\tau/c) + 0.11(C_{L_0} - C_L)^2, \qquad (6\text{-}25)$$

where τ/c is the thickness/chord ratio. The strut drag is estimated as the sum of three terms. The body of the strut has a drag that can be estimated using Eq. (6-25). If the strut has a feathering fairing such that it exerts no lift force to weather, then only the first term of Eq. (6-25) need be taken. The junction of the strut with the foil gives rise to drag effects that depend critically on the fillet or fairing used. The best source of empirical data on this topic is Hoerner (Hoerner, S. F.: *Fluid-Dynamic Drag*, 1958). Lastly, a spray drag arises at the water surface; for sharp-nosed sections a drag coefficient of 0.02 can be taken based on the product of chord and thickness as the reference area. This same term should also be applied to determine the spray drag at the ends of surface-piercing foils.

Now, as a reward for the practical-minded reader who has managed to plough through the foregoing tedious but *very* necessary material, we turn now to the subject of hydrofoil construction. The first problem is the selection of a suitable foil section. For surface-piercing foils, the most appropriate type for sailing applications, the drag at the surface is minimized by using a section having a sharp leading edge. Such sections have an even pressure distribution when operated at low angles of attack and consequently are not prone to ventilation. If the hydrofoils are to be used on a proa, the ultimate choice for high speed, then the foil section must look the same from either direction. The likely choice for both reasons is the *ogival* section (flat on the bottom and a constant radius on top). The maximum possible $\mathscr{L}/\mathscr{D}$ for this apparently simple section is only slightly less than is possible with a blunt section as shown by the curves plotted in Fig. 6-17. In practice, however, the advantage of a blunt-nosed section can only be realized with a deeply submerged foil and then, only if the foil, particularly in the neighbourhood of the leading edge, can be made and finished to a standard unattainable by the amateur constructor.

There is a particularly handy technique for constructing ogival foils that was first brought to my attention by Dave Keiper. In order to machine the foils, a wooden cylinder with an equilateral polygon cross section and a carefully centred metal shaft is made as shown in Fig. 6-18. Bar stock is then mounted on each flat and the lot is then chucked into a lathe and machined to a constant radius. The choice of the number of sides determines the ratio t/c. In order to make a Gö 708 section (an early German glider section) as seems advisable since data is available, an eleven-sided cylinder should be used. For this section, the radius/chord ratio is 1.7.

Aluminium or laminated wood can be used for foil construction, however a much better strength/weight ratio can be achieved by using

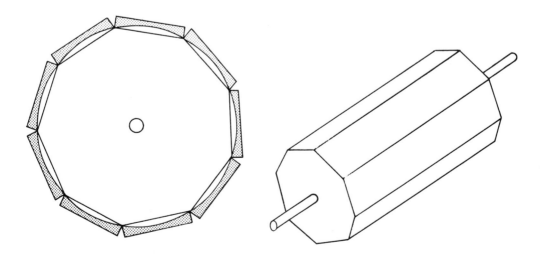

Fig. 6-18. A device for machining ogival foils.

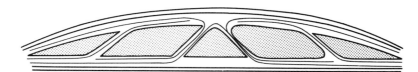

Fig. 6-19. Layup of foam-cored foils.

a PVC foam core (for example, heavy-grade Airex) machined some-what undersize. This can then be cut and layed up using epoxy and Kevlar and carbon fibres. The cuts, as shown in Fig. 6-19, allow a high-strength web to be built between the upper and lower skins. For the finish layer, epoxy-microballoon putty is trowelled on and the foil is machined to final size on the lathe. In this way eleven accurate ogival foil blades, each perhaps four feet long, can be produced simultaneously.

REFERENCES

1 Alexander, A., J. Grogono, and D. Nigg, *Hydrofoil Sailing.* London: Juanita Kalerghi, 1972.

2 Barkla, Hugh, *Sailing on Hydrofoils*, *3*, Association of Northern Univer-sities Sailing Clubs, 1953.

3 Barkla, Hugh, *Yachts and Yachting*, *903* (8 Nov., 1968).

4 Bruce, Edmond and Harry Morss, *Design for Fast Sailing*, (AYRS 82), Hermitage, Berks.: Amateur Yacht Research Society, 1976.

5 Chapman, G. C., *AYRS Airs 7*, 41 (1973).

6 DuCane, Peter, *High Speed Small Craft* (4th ed.) Tuckahoe, N. Y.: John de Graff, Inc., 1973.

7 Hook, C., *Why Sailing Hydrofoils?* Ancient Interface Symposium IV, 1973.

8 Hook, C. and A. C. Kermode, *Hydrofoils.* London: Sir Isaac Pitman & Sons, Ltd., 1967.

9 Marchaj, C. A., *Sailing, Theory and Practice.* New York: Dodd, Meade & Co., 1964.

10 Norwood, J., *Some Thoughts on the Ultimate Yacht*, MIAPH-GP-72.4, University of Miami, 1972.

11 Norwood, J., *Multihulls*, vol. 2, no. 2, 62 (1976).

12 Prandtl, L. and O. G. Tietjens, *Applied Hydro- and Aeromechanics.* New York: Dover Publications, Inc., 1934.

13 *Sailing Hydrofoils* (AYRS 74). Hermitage, Berks.: Amateur Yacht Research Society, 1970.

7 SAFETY AND SEAKEEPING

In this chapter we shall be primarily concerned with the problem of multihull's extreme initial stability and the consequent high com- at sea. Other grave situations may occur, of course. Multihulls may be dismasted in situations where a monohull would not owing to the multihulls extreme initial stability and the consequent high com- pressional loading on the mast owing to gusts. Multihull rudders and boards are similarly more prone to breakage than monohull rudders as a result of the considerably higher speeds attained. These factors must be anticipated in the design. It is, however, the fact that multihulls are stable in the inverted as well as the normal upright position that causes the most concern.

Capsize can be caused by wind, wave, or a combination of the two. It is obvious from our stability studies in Chapter 4 that a large beam, low centre of gravity, and a low aspect rig are all design virtues from the point of view of capsize avoidance. The question of trimaran outrigger (or proa leeward hull) buoyancy is not so straightforward. If the buoyancy is insufficient to support the entire weight of the craft, then the initial stability is reduced and the onset of capsize conditions under sail are more readily apparent as the lee outrigger begins to bury. Under extreme storm conditions the yacht should be relied on to behave as a stable raft and be capable of sliding sideways on a steep wave slope to avoid the breaking crest. Craft with low-buoyancy outriggers do not do this. As the wave heels the boat, the lee outrigger sub- merges and the boat becomes very resistant to sideways motion. Consequently the outrigger can act as a stationary axis about which the crest of the wave will capsize the craft. Any vertical hydrofoil such as a dagger board or leeboard in the outrigger can contribute markedly to the sideward resistance, consequently, these should all be retracted when lying ahull. The same does not necessarily hold true for leeward Bruce foils, however. If the dihedral angle is in the recommended 40-45 degree range, then the flat bottom surface of the foils will become parallel to the sea surface as the boat heels and will provide a sort of water ski on which the boat can move sideward. This will, of course, be more true for the low aspect foils favoured by Bruce and Morss than for high aspect ladder foils. About the only meaningful experience in this area belongs to Dave Keiper who has done many thousands of miles in the Pacific in his hydrofoil trimaran *Williwaw* and has weathered some fairly severe conditions.

The proa configuration optimizes its stability by keeping the heavier hull permanently to windward. In a seaway or under changing wind conditions the danger always exists of being caught aback with the wind on the wrong side. Under these conditions the lateral stability of the proa is then less than that of a catamaran of comparable beam. This must be compensated in the design. During an early trial cruise with *Cheers*, Tom Follett experienced such a windward capsize which was fortunately limited to 90 degrees by the buoyant masts located in the windward hull. Follett was unable to right the boat without outside assistance however. As a cure, Newick installed a sponson or bulge on the windward side as shown in Fig. 7-1. This sponson was designed

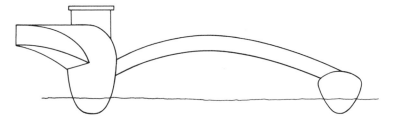

Fig. 7-1. Proa *Cheers* showing windward sponson.

to halt a windward capsize at about 40 degrees where a release of the wind pressure could allow the craft to recover. In a cruising proa, such a bulge could add considerable accommodation space. In a racing machine where weight and windage are at a premium, the sponson could consist of an inflatable outrigger (two Benyon-Tinker 15-foot inflatable catamaran hulls installed transom to transom) connected by short beams to the hull, a sort of deformed trimaran. Another approach to the windward capsize problem for proas is to arrange a mechanism whereby the sheet or sheets are automatically released in the event of wind pressure from the wrong side. The details of such an arrangement will vary from one rig to another, however it should not be a difficult thing to engineer.

The only sort of sheet cleats that should be used are cam cleats which can be released manually by a quick upward tug on the sheet. Piver designed an automatic sheet release as shown in Fig. 7-2 for use on his trimarans. This consists of one or more cam cleats mounted on a base which is hinged on the sail side of the cleat. A length of shock cord is attached to the opposite end of the hinged base and led downward to another small cam cleat. There the tension is adjusted to affect a release at any predetermined sheet tension. This occurs owing to the couple formed between the sheet and the hinge axis. A commercial sheet release has been manufactured by Hepplewhite Marine Ltd. This gear operates by mercury switches at a preset heel angle in either direction and releases the cam cleats magnetically. Unfortunately Hepplewhites have recently discontinued this item. The effectiveness of any type of sheet release gear depends on the ability of the sheet to run free. The use of multifold purchases and winches

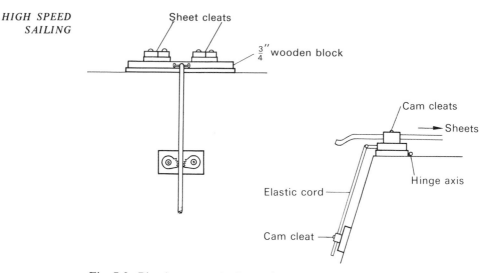

Fig. 7-2. Piver's automatic sheet release gear.

obviously inhibits this ability severely. The pyramid rig offers a great advantage in this regard since only one sheet is involved and for all but the largest rigs, the sheet does not use winches or multifold purchases owing to the nearly balanced nature of the rig. As added insurance, a sharp hand axe should be clip-mounted in the cockpit in order to be able to chop the sheets should all else fail. Drills should be arranged and each crewman should have a predetermined task under such emergency conditions.

Some designers have favoured the use of permanent masthead buoyancy in the form of a fat disc or weathercocking teardrop form. I do not believe this to be a good idea. In the first place, the weight and windage of such a device at the masthead will promote the problem it is designed to cure. Secondly, if the yacht does capsize, the masthead float may well exert such an impulsive force as to break the mast. On balance, such measures probably do more harm than good.

In the event of a capsize, a multihull with a high-volume beam structure such as *Three Cheers* (see Fig. 2-9) will float quite high in the water. By fitting a capsize hatch under one of the bunks such that it is capable of being opened from either side, quick access to or from the hull is provided. Such a capsize hatch is permissable in a trimaran and possibly in a proa, however it is not suitable for a catamaran. A well-designed trimaran has two watertight outriggers to provide ample buoyancy when the hatch is opened and the pressurized bubble of air in the hull is released. Additionally, adequate handholds must be provided on the underside of the beams and on the hull above the waterline. The liferaft and all survival stores must be stowed so as to be readily available with the yacht in the inverted position.

Over the years the AYRS has published many schemes for righting capsized multihulls at sea, however none has worked out except on a trial basis in harbour under ideal conditions. Most of these schemes

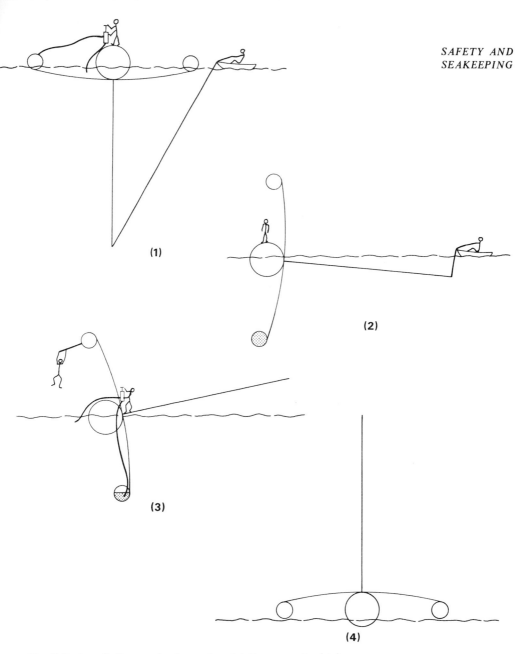

(1)

(2)

(3)

(4)

Fig. 7-3. An oft-discussed scheme for righting a capsized trimaran.

have involved slight variations on the idea shown in Fig. 7-3. Water is pumped into the leeward outrigger and the halyard is used to raise the mast to the 90 degree position from the life raft. The submerged outrigger is then pumped out and at some point wind and wave action are expected to right the craft. The problem with this scheme is that it is difficult to kill the buoyancy of the leeward outrigger and beam structure, especially in a foam sandwich boat. Only a trimaran with cold moulded wooden outriggers and tubular aluminium 81 cross members would have any hope of being righted in this way and then only if the mast had not been broken by the capsize as often happens. For catamarans and proas no righting over the side scheme seems to hold promise.

The first real breakthrough in multihull righting occurred at the World Multihull Symposium in Toronto in 1976 in the form of a discussion and model demonstration by Carlos Jim Ruiz of El Salvador, Central America. Ruiz's idea involves righting over the bows and is

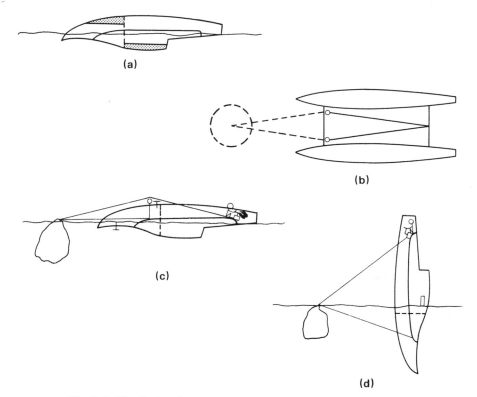

Fig. 7-4. The Ruiz scheme for righting a capsized multihull.

shown in Fig. 7-4. Figure 7-4(a) shows the boat on its back with sufficient foam in the cabin top to cause the craft to float high and offer as dry as possible accommodation in the cabin until the seas subside sufficiently to make a righting attempt. The crosshatched areas represent foam flotation and the vertical dashed line indicates a watertight bulkhead separating the cabin from the bow section. Figure 7-4(b) shows an A-frame of alloy tubing hinged at the leading edge of the forward connecting beam. This A-frame is connected to a water bag at the vertex and pivoted forward over the bow and the bag allowed to fill. A small A-frame is positioned in sockets in the forward beam as shown in (c) and a line is run from the bag attachment point, over the block at the vertex of the small frame to a large winch mounted on the bottom of the rear crossbeam. Valves are opened as shown in the deck and bottom of the bow section(s) to allow water to enter and air to escape as the water bag is winched up. In this way the boat is brought to a vertical position as shown in Fig. 7-4(d). An openable window is fitted in the cabin so as to be just above the waterline in this position in order to allow water to drain from the cabin. In this position the boat is quite stable (as spar buoys are) and the cabin will be dry. Wave action and a little more winching will then put the craft in an upright position. By leaving the two valves in the bow open the foam floatation in the bows will then cause them to self-bail and you are back in business. Note that in this scheme we have not had to depend on the mast which may or may not be broken in the capsize. If the mast is intact, then an inflatable masthead float of small dimensions may be used to assist the righting from (c) to (d). If the mast is lost then the A-frame used to right the boat can subsequently be used to make a jury rig. At the time of this writing (December, 1977) this scheme has not been attempted to right an *unplanned* capsize, however, in my opinion, it stands a very good chance of working.

REFERENCES

1 Follett, Tom, Dick Newick, and Jim Morris, *Project Cheers*. London: Adlard Coles Ltd., 1969.

2 Harris, Robert B., *Racing and Cruising Trimarans*. New York: Charles Scribner's Sons. 1970.

3 Henderson, Richard, *Sea Sense*, Camden, Maine: International Marine Publishing Company, 1972 and London: Adlard Coles Limited.

4 McMullen, Michael, *Multihull Seamanship*. New York: David McKay Company, Inc., 1976.

5 Multihulls, *3*, 24 (1976).

6 Myers, Hugo, *Ocean Racing Multihull Design Considerations*, SNAME New England Sailing Yacht Symposium, New London, Conn. 1976.

7 Various AYRS members, *Multihull Safety Study*, AYRS, 69 (1969).

8 PERFORMANCE PREDICTION

In chapter one we derived an equation for the ratio of boat speed to true wind speed

$$\frac{V_B}{V_T} = \sin \gamma \ \mathrm{ctn} \ \beta - \cos \gamma \qquad (8\text{-}1)$$

where γ and β are the course angles to the true and apparent wind vectors respectively. We want to be able to predict the speed of a boat on any course angle γ subject to a given wind speed V_T, thus we shall consider V_T and γ as known input variables.

The angle β was found to be the sum of the aero- and hydrodynamic drag angles δ_A and δ_H, where

$$\delta_A = \mathrm{arcctn}(\mathscr{L}_A/\mathscr{D}_A),$$
$$\delta_H = \mathrm{arcctn}(\mathscr{L}_H/\mathscr{D}_H). \qquad (8\text{-}2)$$

In order to find V_B (or β), we must therefore calculate the lift and drag of all parts of the boat above the waterline and that of all parts of the boat below the waterline. Let us see what this entails.

The aerodynamic lift can be written as

$$\mathscr{L}_A = \tfrac{1}{2}\rho_A V_A^2 A_S C_{LA} \cos^2 \theta. \qquad (8\text{-}3)$$

The quantity $\tfrac{1}{2}\rho_A = 1.19 \cdot 10^{-3}$ slug/ft^3. The apparent wind speed V_A can be expressed in terms of V_B, V_T and γ,

$$V_A^2 = V_B^2 + V_T^2 + 2V_B V_T \cos \gamma \qquad (8\text{-}4)$$

by applying the law of cosines to the sailing triangle (Fig. 1-1) or, in terms of β, V_T and γ

$$\frac{V_A}{V_T} = \frac{\sin \gamma}{\sin \beta} \qquad (8\text{-}5)$$

by use of the law of sines.

The sail area A_S must be considered in two limiting cases: 1) as a given constant in light to medium winds, and 2) as a function of $1/V_A^2$ in heavy winds where the craft is operated at the limits of its lateral stability. In either case, the stability equations for fore-and-aft or pyramid rigged craft as derived in Chapt. 4 must be invoked.

The lift coefficient is an approximately linear function of the angle of attack up to about 13 degrees or so for very flat sails and 30 degrees for very full ones; C_L decreases for higher angles of attack and reaches zero for $\alpha = 90$ degrees. The detail shape of the curve is a function of the aspect ratio, twist control, presence or absence of fences, rolling motion of the yacht, and a million more little factors that are impossible to take into account analytically.

The $\cos^2 \theta$ term on the end of Eq. (8-3) takes into account heeling. If a pyramid rig is used, then $\cos^2 \theta$ must be replaced by $[\cos^2(\theta + \psi) + \cos^2(\theta - \psi)]/2$ where ψ is the angle of inclination of the pyramid rig ($\psi = 19.5$ degrees for $A = 3$).

The calculation of the aerodynamic drag $\mathcal{D}_A$ is similar except that there is an additional component of drag not associated with the sail

$$\mathcal{D}_A = \tfrac{1}{2}\rho_A V_A^2 A_S(C_{DA} + \varepsilon C_{PA}). \qquad (8\text{-}6)$$

The drag coefficient C_{DA} is composed of frictional, induced, and form-associated components. The quantity ε is the ratio of the area of the spars, rigging, hulls, cabins, etc. to the sail area and C_{PA} is corresponding drag coefficient. Both ε and C_{PA} are sensitive functions of β and the heel angle.

As you can see, the problem is difficult to specify and is highly nonlinear even if all of the specifications could be given. As an indication of the magnitudes of the lift and drag coefficients, a polar plot of C_{LA} versus C_{DA} for a fairly good rig and clean deck layout is given in Fig. 8-1.

The situation with regard to the hydrodynamic lift and drag is also complicated.

$$\mathcal{L}_H = \tfrac{1}{2}\rho_H V_B^2(A_P C_{LP} + A_K C_{LK}) \qquad (8\text{-}7)$$

Here $\tfrac{1}{2}\rho_H = 0.995$ slug/ft^3. In order to find the optimum keel area, A_K (considered to be variable) one must equate $\mathcal{L}_H$ to F_y which leads to further complication. The calculation of $\mathcal{D}_H = R$ is also fraught with uncertainty. As we saw in Chapt. 2, resistance arises owing to a very complex set of phenomena. Even though I have considerable faith in the Havelock-Castles equation as a qualitative tool, I would not expect its quantitative predictions to be consistently accurate for all sorts of hulls under all sorts of sailing conditions.

In a word, the sailing problem does not yield to a direct frontal assault. It is a 'messy' problem. This is not to say that nothing can be done with it, however.

Hugo Myers takes zero order estimates of the leeway angle, heel angle and boat speed for a given γ and V_T. Using the estimated V_B, the sailing triangle is solved for β_1 and V_{A_1}. This value of V_A then goes into the heeling equation to derive an improved value of $\theta = \theta_1$. Using V_{A_1}, θ_1, and β_1 the equations $F_x = \mathcal{D}_H$ and $F_y = \mathcal{L}_H$ are solved simultaneously by an iterative technique to derive a true wind speed V_{T_1} and improved leeway angle λ_1 and boat speed V_{B_1}. The heeling angle θ_1 and boat speed V_{B_1} are then corrected by multiplying by V_T/V_{T_1} and the whole process is repeated to find a V_{T_2}, V_{T_3}, etc. until the ratio with V_T approaches unity and V_B approaches a value which is found to be in reasonable agreement with measured values.

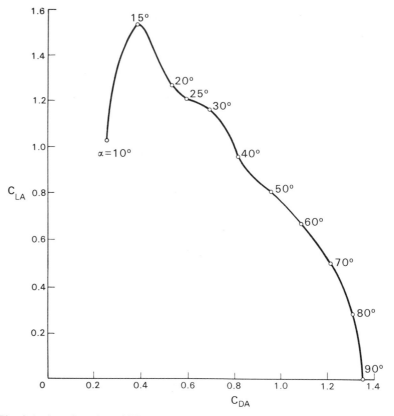

Fig. 8-1. A polar plot of lift versus drag coefficients for an efficient rig on a clean hull.

This works pretty well so long as the coefficients can be estimated. It is nearly impossible to use a computer program like this to formulate general principles; only specific answers to specific questions can be given.

We note from Fig. 1-7 that the ice yacht maintains an almost constant value of β up to $\gamma = 100$ degrees or so. Since very fast craft tend to operate at constant β, let us look at this case. Equation (8-1) becomes

$$\frac{V_B}{V_T} = \Psi \sin \gamma - \cos \gamma, \qquad (8\text{-}8)$$

where

$$\Psi = \operatorname{ctn} \beta = \text{const.} \qquad (8\text{-}9)$$

In Fig. 8-2 we show polar plots of V_B/V_T as a function of γ for several different values of $\beta = \text{const.}$ These curves are circles of radius

$$r = \tfrac{1}{2} \csc \beta \qquad (8\text{-}10)$$

all passing through the origin and centred along the radial line

$$\gamma = 90° + \beta. \qquad (8\text{-}11)$$

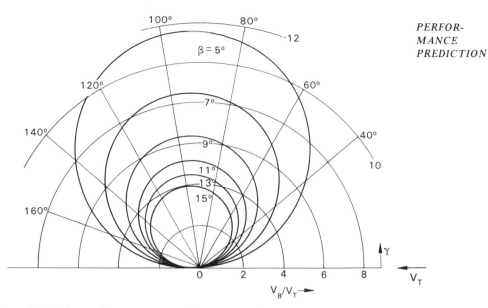

Fig. 8-2. Polar performance curves for constant β.

The maximum speed to windward is achieved at a course angle

$$\gamma_w = 45° + \beta/2 \tag{8-12}$$

and the speed attained to windward along this course is

$$\frac{V_B}{V_T} \cos \gamma_W = \tfrac{1}{2}(\csc \beta - 1). \tag{8-13}$$

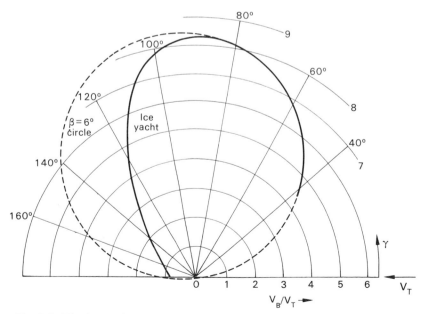

Fig. 8-3. The ice yacht as a constant β sailing craft.

87

The maximum downward speed is made at a course angle

$$\gamma_D = 135° + \beta/2 \tag{8-14}$$

and the corresponding downwind speed is

$$\frac{V_B}{V_T} \cos \gamma_D = \tfrac{1}{2}(\csc \beta + 1) \tag{8-15}$$

(A derivation of equations (8-10) to (8-15) is presented in Appendix C.) In Fig. 8-3 we show the polar curve for the ice boat plotted with the circle for $\beta = 6$ degrees. No other type of sailing craft approximates constant β.

In analyzing the performance of less efficient sailing craft we shall equate the x-component of the vector equation

$$\mathbf{F}_A = -\mathbf{F}_H \tag{8-16}$$

Using Eq. (2-23) for R in place of $\mathcal{D}_H$ and using Eq. (8-4) to eliminate $V_A{}^2$ from F_x. We find

$$V_B{}^2 + V_T{}^2 + 2V_B V_T \cos \gamma = \frac{aWV_B{}^2}{\tfrac{1}{2}\rho_A A_S LC_x}$$

or

$$\left(\frac{1 - v_1}{v_1}\right)\left(\frac{V_B}{V_T}\right)^2 - 2 \cos \gamma \left(\frac{V_B}{V_T}\right) - 1 = 0, \tag{8-17}$$

where

$$v_1 = \frac{\rho_A C_x}{2a} \cdot \frac{A_S L}{W}. \tag{3-18}$$

Equation (8-17) has as its solution,

$$\frac{V_B}{V_T} = \frac{v_1}{1 - v_1}\left(\cos \gamma + \sqrt{\cos^2 \gamma + \frac{1 - v_1}{v_1}}\right). \tag{8-19}$$

In order to interpret this equation we need to know the order of magnitude of v_1. For boats of interest to us we find that v_1 is generally much smaller than one. In this limit

$$\frac{V_B}{V_T} \approx \sqrt{v_1} = \text{const} \sqrt{\frac{A_S L}{W}}. \tag{8-20}$$

In a recent paper, Kelsall and Shuttleworth reported that

$$\frac{V_B}{V_T} = 0.4 \sqrt{\frac{A_S L}{W}} \tag{8-21}$$

provides an approximation to V_B/V_T for $V_T = 10$ knots as calculated from the IOMR equations to within less than five percent. Thus Eq. (8-21) provides a useful tool with which to compare the performance potential of various designs.

Now let us consider a simplified version of the heeling equation, approximately valid at the point where the windward hull lifts out

$$\bar{y}W = h(\tfrac{1}{2}\rho_A V_A^2 A_S C_y). \qquad (8\text{-}22)$$

Again we use Eq. (8-4) to eliminate V_A^2. We obtain

$$V_B^2 + 2V_B V_T \cos \gamma + V_T^2 - v_2 = 0 \qquad (8\text{-}23)$$

where

$$v_2 = \frac{2}{\rho_A C_y} \cdot \frac{\bar{y}W}{hA_S} \qquad (8\text{-}24)$$

Equation (8-23) has as its solution

$$V_B = \sqrt{v_2 - (1 - \cos^2 \gamma)V_T^2} - V_T \cos \gamma \qquad (8\text{-}25)$$

For $\gamma = 90$ degrees, the near-optimum course for sailing at the limit, Eq. (8-25) reduces to

$$V_B = \sqrt{v_2 - V_T^2} \qquad (8\text{-}26)$$

This equation tells us what maximum boat speed can be attained on a beam reach in a given V_T before you sail yourself over on your own apparent wind. If we take $C_y = 1$ as before and eliminate V_T using Eq. (8-21), we find for $V_{B,\,max}$

$$V_{B,\,max} = 6.86 \sqrt{\frac{WL\bar{y}}{h(0.16A_S L + W)}}, \text{ knots.} \qquad (8\text{-}27)$$

In Table 8-1 we have listed the measured parameters of several British multihulls. In the last three columns are given V_B/V_T as specified by Eq. (8-21) and $V_{B,\,max}$ in knots together with the true wind speed necessary to reach this speed.

Table 8-1. Performance parameters for several British multihulls.

Name	L	W	A_S	h	$\bar{y}$	V_B/V_T	$V_{B,\,max}$ (kn)	V_T (kn)
TRIFLE	39.67	7936	807	21.0	13.5	0.803	27.0	33.6
ROQUOIS 204	27.14	6470	463	13.6	6.57	0.557	21.7	39.0
CRODA WAY	32.03	6028	618	17.2	12.12	0.725	26.4	36.4
T	27.64	7699	814	18.0	13.1	0.684	25.4	37.1
TAHITI BILL	36.70	13693	876	21.0	8.27	0.613	22.2	36.2
CHEERS	43.25	8310	964	21.6	13.27	0.896	26.3	29.4
GB III	71.07	42748	2709	35.7	18.87	0.849	32.1	37.8

The designer and rule deviser both need to know how changes in the various parameters of a yacht affect its performance. The IOMR under which multihull yachts are presently rated seems to be an accurate performance indicator. The rule does not measure overall beam or outrigger length and therefore encourages exploitation of this loophole for trimarans and proas. Unfortunately, the rule is too complex to allow the designer to optimize a specific design with its use.

Kelsall has suggested that the IOMR rating might be replaced by a time correction factor defined by

$$\text{TCF} = 0.5\sqrt{\frac{A_S L}{W}} = 1.25\,\frac{V_B}{V_T}.\qquad(8\text{-}28)$$

If a race is run under heavy average wind conditions, then the rule should also feature a heavy weather factor that includes the specification of overall beam and the keel-to-sail height h. Similarly, in light weather the ratio of sail area to wetted surface is important and some sort of factor such as $\sqrt{A_S/LB}$ becomes important. Work is in progress at this writing to define a rule along these lines.

REFERENCES

1 Bruce, Edmond and Harry Morss, *Design for Fast Sailing*, (AYRS 82), Hermitage, Berks: Amateur Yacht Research Society, 1976.

2 *International Offshore Multihull Rule*, London: International Yacht Racing Union.

3 Kelsall, Derek and John Shuttleworth, RYA Speed Sailing Symposium, 1977; *Multihull International*, *111*, 67 (1977).

4 Myers, Hugo; Second SNAME Chesapeake Sailing Yacht Symposium, Annapolis, Md. 1975.

9 CATAMARANS

Catamarans enjoy a performance advantage over trimarans in heavy winds in that they can fly the windward hull and thereby sail on one hull with less resistance. This advantage can be realized only in the daysailing sizes where the crew weight is useful as mobile ballast and capsize is not a serious matter.

Daysailing catamaran racing is carried out in three classes in which the only restriction is overall length, overall beam, and total sail area as shown in Table 9-1. In addition there is a D class at a length of 30 feet and a sail area of 500 ft^2, however this is limited mostly to California. The serious international competition is in C class. A series of races known as the Little America's Cup is run periodically and is hotly contested. In class B, the Tornado designed by Rodney March is an Olympic class. Except for minor variations in rudders, all class B racing is done in similar boats. Class C is a one-off class and it is here that the innovation, mostly in sail rigs, is taking place. Early craft carried sloop rigs, however they were soon eclipsed by catamarans carrying a single mainsail. The cost and speed both went up with the appearance of the wing mast, a rotating airfoil having from ten to fifty percent of the total sail area with a fully battened soft sail attached to the trailing edge. The latest development is the solid wing sail which looks very much like a vertical half-wing from a glider. These wingsail craft have been handicapped in light airs by the extra weight of the wing, however the increasing use of exotic materials such as carbon fibres is tilting the balance in favour of the wingsail.

Table 9-1

Class	LOA, ft.	BOA, ft.	A_S, ft^2	Crew
A	18	7.5	150	1
B	20	10	235	2
C	25	14	300	2

In order to reverse the camber of a wingsail upon tacking, a series   91 of rigid flaps at the trailing edge are actuated. In 1977, designer Dave Hubbard introduced a solid wing on Tony DiMauro's *Patient Lady III* that can be warped to produce camber and twist in either direction. This wing is just under 40 feet long and weighs about 230 pounds. The framing and leading edge are plywood and carbon fibre and a Mylar covering is used. This warpable wing has proven very effective downwind.

What about hydrofoil application to daysailing catamarans? The most successful work to date has been done on A and B class boats by Phillip Hansford and James Grogono. Grogono's boat *Icarus* is basically a standard Tornado. The hydrofoil system has been under continuous development since the late 1960's. The first set of foils were 45 degree dihedral, used a 9 percent ogival section, and featured a large foil at the stern and a small foil at the bow of each hull. Steering was by standard rudders with extra long blades. The bow foil was operated at a 4° angle of attack and the stern foil at 1° for pitch damping (see Chapt. 6). As development proceeded, the foils were made smaller to raise the takeoff speed and improve hull-borne handling. Next the bow foils were mounted on pintles and used for steering. The handling at speed on foils was reported to be sensitive and stable.

Phillip Hansford's class A catamaran *Mayfly* (see Fig. 6-11) has an aeroplane foil configuration. The main load is carried by the front foils which are mounted on an extension of the forward crossbeam. The dihedral angle is 40 degrees. The rear foil is a T unit mounted at the bottom of the single centre-mounted rudder. The upper and lower surfaces of the foil are cambered equally and set at zero angle of attack. This unit thus acts to keep the boat in level flight. The overall beam of the front foils is about 14 feet, only a little less than the length and the compensation of the heeling torque is very nearly complete. The leeway angle adjusts itself so that the windward foil is producing some negative lift. In sailing trials in quite strong winds, the boat shows no tendency to heel. In order to stabilize against pitching instability, the bow foils were set at a 4° angle of attack which would seem to be unfortunate since the lift-to-drag ratio is not optimal at this angle and the foil carries about 65 percent of the load. In fast sailing the helmsman must shift himself back to the extreme stern in order to assist the rear foil in keeping the bows up. *Mayfly's* success has been phenomenal. In the 1972 John Player Speed Sailing event at Portland Harbour, Weymouth, *Mayfly* did 16.4 knots. By 1975 this was raised to 19.4 knots over the one-way 500 metre course. In 1977 she was sold to Ben Wynn who posted a new class A record of 21.2 knots.

By comparison, *Icarus* is under-compensated and heels to a fair degree. *Icarus* appears to operate at a smaller leeway angle than *Mayfly*, hence the weather foil probably exerts little if any negative lift. Pitching stability has seemed to be a problem on some occasions. She has, under ideal conditions, sailed at about 26 knots. The class B record established at Weymouth by *Icarus* stands at 20.7 knots as of 1976, less than the class A record. In establishing this record *Icarus* used an aeroplane foil system of the same type as *Mayfly's*. Another catamaran, *Bluey* built by George Chapman also uses *Mayfly* foils. One reason that *Icarus* and *Bluey* have not equaled *Mayfly's* success

92

is that they are somewhat heavy. *Mayfly*, less crew, weighs only
130-150 pounds. Another reason is that both of the other boats heel.

In the large sizes suitable for offshore sailing, catamarans are quite attractive as cruising boats, offering as they do accommodation in both hulls and in a deckhouse which, in sizes 40 feet and up, usually has standing headroom. For offshore racing with a crew of one or two, the catamaran has not been as popular as the trimaran.

Catamarans can be made flexible or rigid. The fast rigid catamarans are typified by such CSK designs as *Seasmoke* and *Tahiti Bill*. *Seasmoke* with a rated waterline length of 49.44 feet weighs 24499 pounds and carries a crew of nine. *Tahiti Bill*, ten feet shorter, weighs 13693 pounds. Both of these yachts are heavy and narrow by modern standards. James Wharram has designed a series of flexible cruising catamarans which have an enviable safety record. Flexible racers have been less successful. Rod Macalpine-Downie designed *Mirrorcat* for the 1966 Round Britain Race using two 40 foot Comanche hulls connected by aluminium tubing. All accommodation is in the hulls and the deck consists only of trampoline webbing. The boat was not successful in this race and was eventually retired to cruising use with a strengthened connector system. *British Oxygen*, another Macalpine-Downie design with structural advice from the British aerospace industry was a sort of 70 foot Tornado connected by four large alloy mast extrusions. She was built in 1974 and won the 1974 Round Britain Race, narrowly beating the 46 foot trimaran *Three Cheers*. Renamed *Kriter III*, the big catamaran was lost in the storm experienced on the northern route in the 1976 Royal Western Observer Singlehanded Transatlantic Race. According to Jean-Yves Terlain, her skipper, she rose from burying her bows in a large wave with the forward beam broken. This led to the progressive failure of the other beams and the boat broke up and sank shortly after Terlain was taken off.

In a trimaran, the mast is stepped in the hull. In a catamaran it must be stepped on a crossbeam. With a conventional rig, the large stresses imposed on the beam structure by the mast, stays, and shrouds complicate the structural picture considerably and limit the overall beam. It is therefore much more important for an offshore catamaran to use a rig with *self-contained* stresses such as the pyramid rig than it is for a trimaran. Let us look at the question of hull connections more closely.

In Chapt. 3 we found that the bending strains are the most severe ones that the beam encounters. This strain was given in Eq. (3-1) as

$$\sigma_{max} = \frac{Wlh}{I} \tag{9-1}$$

where W is the weight of the boat, l is the length of the beam, h is the half depth of the beam, and I is the areal moment of inertia given for a hollow rectangular beam by

$$I = \tfrac{2}{3}a[h^3 - (h - \tau)^3] \tag{9-2}$$

where a is the width of the beam and τ is the skin thickness. For beams of large cross section $h \gg \tau$ and Eq. (9-2) reduces to

$$I \approx 2ah^2\tau \tag{9-3}$$

and Eq. (9-1) can therefore be written as

$$\sigma_{max} = \frac{1}{2} \frac{Wl}{ah\tau} \tag{9-4}$$

The weight of the beam which we shall assume to taper is given approximately by

$$W_B = l(a + 2h)\tau v \tag{9-5}$$

where v is the weight density of the beam skin (specific gravity times 62.4 lb/ft^3). Eliminating the skin thickness τ from Eq. (9-5) with the use of Eq. (9-4), we find

$$\frac{W_B}{W} = l^2 \cdot \frac{v}{\sigma_{max}} \cdot \frac{a + 2h}{2ah}, \tag{9-6}$$

from which we find for the beam length l

$$l = \sqrt{\frac{W_B}{W} \cdot \frac{\sigma_{max}}{v} \cdot \left(\frac{2ah}{a + 2h}\right)}. \tag{9-7}$$

This is a very interesting and useful formula. The quantity σ_{max}/v, wholly a function of the material of which the beams are constructed, has the dimension of a length. This number is found from Table 3-1 to be $2.04 \cdot 10^4$ ft for glass cloth in polyester and $1.15 \cdot 10^5$ ft for carbon fibres in epoxy. The quantity in parenthesis in Eq. (9-7) also has the dimensions of a length and takes into account geometrical factors. Since, for otherwise similar boats, the geometrical factor is proportional to the length L, thus the beam length can only increase with $\sqrt{L}$. This agrees with our observation of nature where large animals are stocky and insects are delicate.

Catamarans should be designed to exploit their possible natural advantages over a trimaran, namely lower windage and consequently, better performance to windward. By using a pyramid rig the structural problem will be alleviated to the point that a slight weight saving over a comparable trimaran may be realized. The overall length to overall beam ratio for catamarans is typically about 2 : 1. Conservative estimates using Eq. (9-7) suggest that lower length-to-beam ratios are possible in a pyramid rigged catamaran without paying a penalty in weight. The result is an enhancement of the quantity $\sqrt{A_S L/W}$ and top speed capability. The suggested configuration of such a catamaran is shown in Fig. 9-1.

This catamaran, depending upon the size, would feature accommodation for 1-3 crew in the central pod. Leeway resistance is provided by hydraulically operated leeboards on the inner side of the hulls. The rig would use an aspect ratio of about four with fences at the foot. At the present time I would not attempt to incorporate hydrofoils on such a catamaran. For a fifty foot boat, hydrofoils would not offer a theoretical advantage for speeds less than 20 knots and the additional weight would offset the advantage. As hydrofoil development unfolds, I remain open on this question, however.

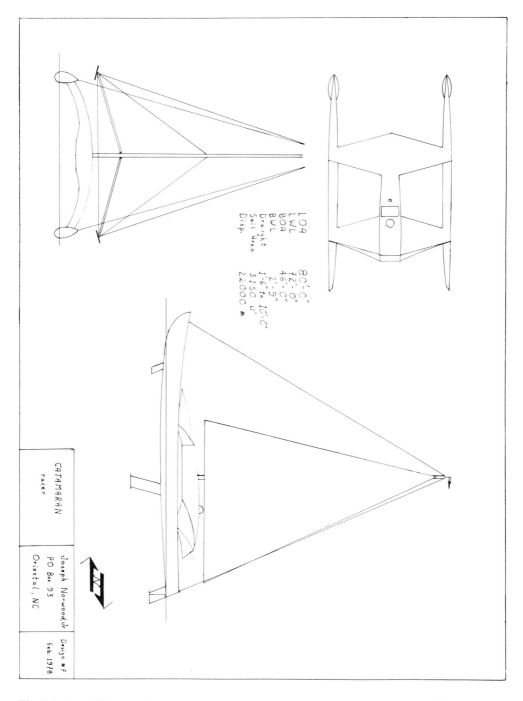

LOA   80'-0"
LWL   72'-0"
BOA   46'-0"
BWL   2'-9"
Draught   1'-6" to 10'-0"
Sail Area   3150 □'
Disp.   22000 #

CATAMARAN
racer

Joseph Norwood, Jr.
PO Box 93
Oriental, NC

Design #7
Feb. 1978

Fig. 9-1. An offshore racing catamaran.

REFERENCES

1 Alexander, Alan; James Grogono, and Donald Nigg, *Hydrofoil Sailing.* London: Juanita Kalerghi, 1972.

2 Cotter, Edward F., *Multihull Sailboats.* New York: Crown Publishers, Inc., 1971.

3 Knights, Jack, *Sail,* 7, No. 12, 70 (1976).

4 McMullen, Michael, *Multihull Seamanship.* New York: David McKay Company, Inc. (1976).

5 Mason, Charles, *Sail,* 8, No. 12, 70 (1977).

6 *Multihull International,* 102, 137 (1976).

10 TRIMARANS

Trimarans have certain natural advantages over catamarans. Let us examine them. In Fig. 10-1a we show a schematic trimaran with the cross-hatched area showing the lateral weight concentration. In some designs the outriggers are also used for accommodation, however we do not consider these charter-type vessels as high-speed craft. Figure 10-1b, c, & d shows three variations of the weight distribution in catamarans. Small catamarans carry all their weight on deck and not in the hulls [see (b)]; they obviously have a very high centre of gravity

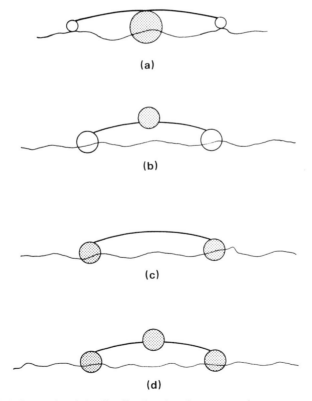

(a)

(b)

(c)

(d)

Fig. 10-1. Lateral weight distribution in trimarans and catamarans.   97

(large $\bar{z}$) which has an adverse affect on lateral stability, Figure 10-1(c) shows a catamaran with accommodation only in the hulls such as *Mirrorcat*. Unfortunately all such craft have been flexible. Figure 10-1(d) shows a catamaran with accommodation in the hulls and a large deckhouse such as *Seasmoke*. All this space creates a sound structure, but the temptation to fill it with weighty items and large crews has been overwhelming. Thus trimarans have the advantage of having lower centre of gravity (smaller $\bar{z}$) and a smaller moment of inertia about the longitudinal roll axis. This smallness of the moment of inertia when coupled with large beam and very low DLR outriggers, will give very high stability without a lot of jerky roll motion. It also makes it much easier for the boat to come about, assuming that the ends of the hull are kept light and the outriggers are rockered somewhat.

In light airs or on downward courses the trimaran can effectively be sailed on one hull; the drag of the outriggers is negligible. In light airs, speeds are such that friction and hence wetted surface are important in determining the resistance. The wetted surface of an arrangement of hulls, all having the same length and prismatic coefficient, increases as the square root of the number of hulls. This can be shown easily using Eqs. (2-20) and (2-22) which can be rewritten for our purpose as

$$A_W = nc_1 B, \tag{10-1}$$

and

$$c_2 = nB^2, \tag{10-2}$$

where c_1 and c_2 are constants and n is the number of hulls. Eliminating B, the beam of an individual hull, between these two equations, we find

$$A_W = c_1 \sqrt{c_2 n}, \tag{10-3}$$

which proves the point. The catamaran can only get onto one hull when near the limits of its stability.

In general, the structural problems are somewhat less severe with a trimaran as compared with a catamaran owing to the fact that weight in the trimaran is all concentrated in one spot rather than being spread over both hulls and the deck as in a catamaran. The steering system is much less complicated since only one rudder is required in the trimaran and the installation of inboard auxilliary power is also easier.

The trimaran has less over-water span of its beams and these can be well arched for wave clearance. In the catamaran the clearance must be minimal in order to afford a minimum wing thickness of 3 to 5 feet in the centre for accommodation and still keep low windage. Low windage and lower overall weight are the sole potential advantages of a catamaran over a trimaran and these advantages are only likely to be realized in *very* large craft. Using exotic materials in the beams and hulls, an overall DLR of perhaps 20 could be achieved with sufficient margin of strength. For L less than 70 feet the trimaran gains advantage becoming a somewhat better overall performer in the under 50 feet size until the catamaran regains the

decisive advantage at about $L = 30$ feet. In this opinion, I am
excluding flexible racing catamarans which, at least in the larger sizes,
I do not consider structurally sound.

In Chapt. 9 we found a scaling relation, Eq. (9-7) that told us that the
overall beam of a catamaran must scale as $\sqrt{L}$ unless the cross
section of the beams is increased more than proportionally. Using
available data, we find that the overall displacement-length ratio of
cold moulded epoxy-encapsulated racing trimarans is given approximately by

$$\text{DLR} = \frac{220}{\sqrt{L}}, \tag{10-4}$$

from which the weight in pounds is found as

$$W = 0.5L^{2.5}. \tag{10-5}$$

This type of construction is the best for racing craft at present, not
because its strength/weight figure is the best one can do, but because
its stiffness/weight *is*. This, of course, is quite important in order to
keep a taut forestay. Using a self-stressed pyramid rig, GRP foam
sandwich construction becomes optimal. In a catamaran, exotic
materials should be used in the hull connecting structure. In the
trimaran, carbon fibre in epoxy should be used in the outriggers
as well as in the beams.

We now have the information we need to see how speed scales with
size. If the overall beam scales with the square root of L as implied
by Eq. (9-7) for proportional increase in the cross section of the
connectors, then the weight scales as $L^{2.5}$ and the ratio V_B/V_T defined
by Eq. (8-20) scales as $\sqrt{L}$. The maximum possible speed defined by
Eq. (8-27) remains almost constant with change of scale, however.
If the hull connector cross section is increased by greater than L^2 in
order to cause the overall beam to scale linearly, then the weight will
go up approximately as L^3 and V_B/V_T will be approximately invariant
and the upper speed limit will increase as $\sqrt{L}$.

An example of a trimaran in the 50 foot size range is shown in
Fig. 10-2. The lateral plane is supplied by the dagger-type skeg and a
pair of leeboards on either side of the hull.

Hydrofoil application to offshore trimarans can definitely be contemplated at the present time. Aeroplane and canard configurations
both appear to be feasible. With the canard configuration, experience
has shown that the bow foil should carry about 15 percent of the
weight and the Bruce foils about 85 percent. In this way the higher
angle of attack of the bow foil and its consequent less than optimal
$\mathscr{L}/\mathscr{D}$ has only a small degrading effect on the overall drag angle of
the system. The outriggers on a hydrofoil trimaran may be somewhat
smaller than those intended for an ordinary trimaran. Careful calculations must be made for the loading of these outriggers at sub-flying
speeds in order to ensure that the DLR does not attain such a value
as to build up a wave resistance hump. The foils should be designed
so that the bow lifts out first. This will lead to an increased angle of
attack on the Bruce foils and cause them to lift the stern smoothly

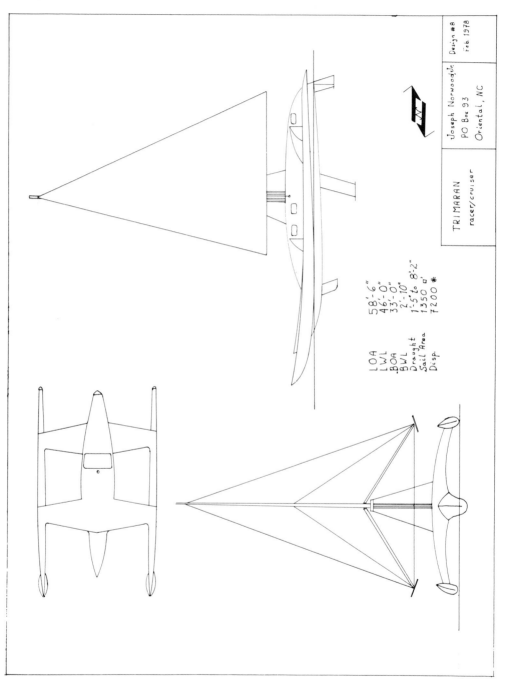

Fig. 10-2. A racing trimaran.

to bring the boat to level flight. The horizontal axis about which the boat pivots in pitch will be somewhat ahead of the bow. This arrangement is very stable. It is important, however to use a bow foil with ample reserve foil area above the foil-borne waterline in order to cope with head seas.

On paper, the canard configuration looks best. The overall drag angle is lower owing to the load distribution and the pitching stability is superior. On the other hand we are faced with the fact of *Mayfly*'s undeniable success with the aeroplane configuration.

Eric Tabarly, a man who must always be taken seriously, is presently (1978) involved in the planning of a 59 foot aeroplane trimaran. This is shown in Fig. 10-3. This boat, to be christened *Pen Duick VII* will be of aluminium construction, albeit of a rather special sort known as an integrated structure system. In this scheme the alloy plates are milled to various thicknesses in order to reduce unneeded weight to a minimum. The entire boat is planned to weigh

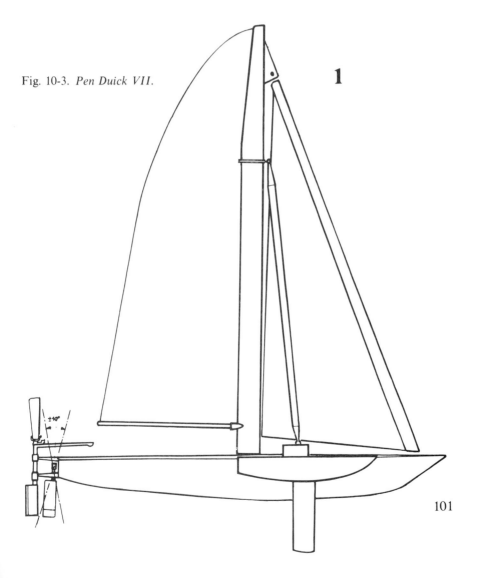

Fig. 10-3. *Pen Duick VII.*

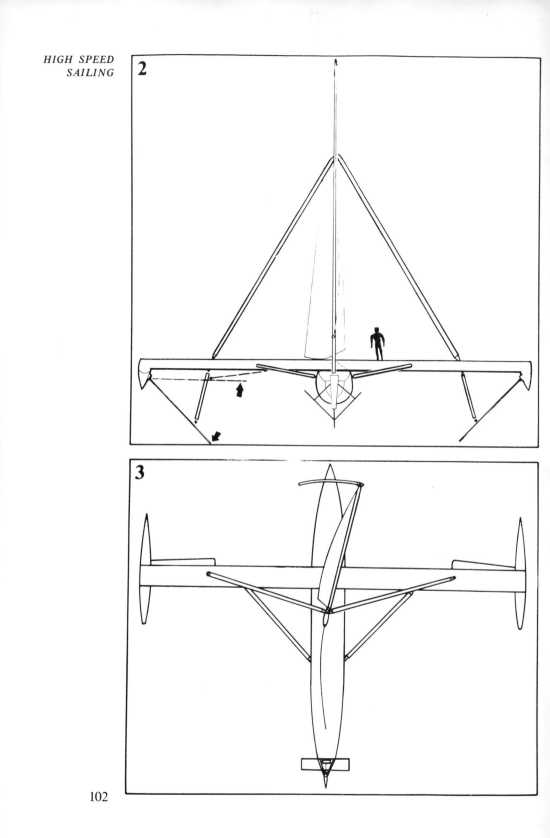

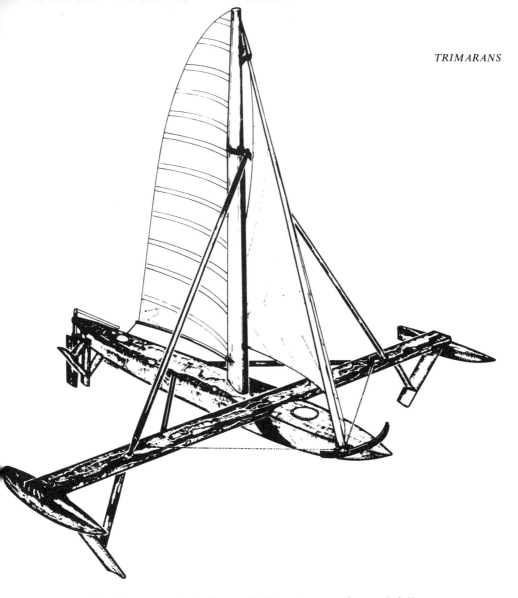

12100 pounds. The span of the beam linking the two forward foils is 66 feet, 7 feet greater than the length. These foils can be set at any dihedral angle up to 45 degrees and serve at zero heel angle to cancel almost completely the heeling torque. The stern foil which serves as rudder and longitudinal trim adjuster will probably carry about 35 percent of the weight with the remaining 65 percent borne by the Bruce foils. Propulsive power is developed by a 2150 ft^2 sloop rig mounted on a 59 foot rotating wing mast. This mast has no shrouds but is supported by two tubular struts to the main beam. This structure is unusual in that it puts the mast into tension rather than compression. Model tests by the Higher National School of Aeronautics at Poiters has indicated that the boat should lift onto its foils at a speed of 12 knots after which a speed of 20-25 knots should be attainable with very little extra effort. Tabarly has been testing a 103

20 foot version offshore and reckons that if he can keep the big boat foil-borne for 5 or 6 days, he stands a good chance of being able to make a singlehanded Atlantic crossing in 15 days.

At the time of writing, the only hydrofoil sailing craft to have crossed oceans successfully is David Keiper's *Williwaw*. This yacht has a trimaran configuration and was designed initially as a hydrofoil craft. *Williwaw* has an overall length of 31 feet and weighs about 2100 pounds empty. The aluminium hydrofoils account for about 400 pounds of this total. The boat is rigged as a sloop with a sail area of 380 ft^2. The hydrofoil configuration is neither canard nor aeroplane but a four-foil combination. The photo of Fig. 10-4 showing *Williwaw* with foils retracted shows the layout. The small outriggers shown were later replaced by larger ones. The bow foil is a single blade of 6 inch chord that spans the boat. The minimum dihedral angle is 30 degrees.

Fig. 10-4. *Williwaw* with all four foils retracted.

The stern foil is a three-rung ladder which combines the functions of
lifter and rudder. The lateral foils are four-rung ladders with a dihedral
angle of 35 degrees. Heeling torque is compensated at a heel angle
of 5°-10° which usually suffices to lift the windward dihedral foil clear
of the water. The hydrofoil configuration when sailing is a sort of reverse
proa configuration with two foils to windward on the hull at a distance
of 26 feet apart and a single dihedral ladder foil to leeward 10 feet
from the symmetry axis. In practice, everything works together very
well.

Williwaw's conception began in 1963. She was built in 1966, first
became foil-borne in April, 1968, and underwent her first trials offshore
in May of the following year. In September of 1970 she made a 16 day
passage from Sausalito, California to Kahului Harbour, Maui under
disadvantageous conditions. Since then *Williwaw* has circumnavigated

Fig. 10-5. *Williwaw* foil-borne at sea.

the Pacific, cruising 20,000 miles between California and New Zealand.

Williwaw is designed to lift off at a speed $V_B = 12$ knots in winds of 13 knots or greater. At takeoff the horizontal projection of the hydrofoil area is about 12 ft^2. The boat operates at a minimal leeway angle except during sharp gusts. The original outriggers had a buoyancy capability of only 600 pounds each. It was found necessary to increase this in two steps to a bit more than 2000 pounds each for take-off in gusty conditions. The bow foil has a forward sweep angle of 10 degrees and the lateral foils a forward sweep angle of 14 degrees. This causes the water encountering the struts at high speed to climb the struts and very effectively prevents the onset of ventilation effects. Keiper has also found it advantageous to add torpedo shapes at the junction of foil blades and struts to alleviate a mild ventilation problem there.

Williwaw is fast under ideal conditions and has flown at better than 20 knots. Her offshore passages have not been remarkable for their speed although stability and seakeeping are greatly enhanced. So far as future development is concerned, *Williwaw* has shown that fixed high aspect ladder foils are a viable proposition for an off-shore sailing machine. David Keiper is a real pioneer and we all owe him a great debt of appreciation. Figure 10-5 shows *Williwaw* foil-borne at sea.

REFERENCES

1 Alexander, Alan; James Grogono, and Lonald Nigg, *Hydrofoil Sailing*. London: Juanita Kalerghi, 1972.

2 Barrault, Jean-Michel, *Sail, 8*, 88 (September, 1977).

3 Clarke, D. H., *Trimarans*. London: Adlard Coles, Ltd, 1969.

4 Cotter, Edward F., *Multihull Sailboats*. New York: Crown Publishers, Inc., 1971.

5 Gougeon, Meade and Ty Knoy, *The Evolution of Modern Sailboat Design*. New York: Winchester Press, 1973.

6 Harris, Robert B., *Racing and Cruising Trimarans*. New York: Charles Scribner's Sons, 1970.

7 Keiper, David, AYRS, *74* (Sailing Hydrofoils) (1970); AYRS *Airs, 11*, 34 (1975); AYRS, *83B*, 36 (1976); AYRS, *85B*, 44 (1976).

8 McMullen, Michael, *Multihull Seamanship*. New York: David McKay Company, Inc., 1976.

9 *Yachts and Yachting, 58*, 93 (26 Dec., 1975).

11 PROAS

Proas represent an approach to sailing that is, for the most part, foreign to Western experience. As a result, this type of multihull has not been explored in terms of modern materials and technology to anything like the extent that catamarans and trimarans have.

The flying proa originated in Micronesia and reached its highest development in the Mariana Islands in the fourteenth or fifteenth centuries. These craft were built in lengths of 70 feet and more and, driven by woven pandanus sails, could sustain speeds of 20 knots on a reach under favourable conditions. During the time that Spain occupied the area, proas were used to carry mail between the Caroline, Mariana, and Philippine Island groups. One of these craft is said to have made the 1700 mile run from Guam to Manila in 6 days.

The drawing of a Marianas flying proa in Fig. 11-1 is a composite of information obtained from historical sources and private communication with Professor Edwin Doran of Texas A & M University. The hull is asymmetric with the curved side to windward. The outrigger is a solid log of considerable weight and has little reserve of buoyancy. If caught aback, the outrigger is rapidly driven under and a capsize ensues. These craft were sailed by large and agile crews who arranged themselves to windward along the connecting structure in order to keep the log flying just clear of the waves, hence the name flying proa.

It is clear that in adapting the proa for western yachtsmen, often sailing shorthanded, that some modification to the concept is necessary. The first step in this direction was taken in 1967 when Dick Newick launched *Cheers*. In *Cheers*, the accommodation, the schooner rig, and the rudders and lateral plane are all carried in the windward hull. The leeward hull is identical to the windward hull to the sheer; its displacement at rest is only about half that of the windward hull, however. This craft was highly successful and took a third place in the 1968 OSTAR against much larger and more costly competition.

The *Cheers* configuration (hull and rig to windward and a buoyant outrigger to leeward) was termed an 'Atlantic proa'. Since then Kelsall has built two Atlantic proas, *Sidewinder* and *Lillian*, however neither has enjoyed any racing success to speak of. In the case of *Sidewinder* the daggerboards were placed in the outrigger which led to a balance 107

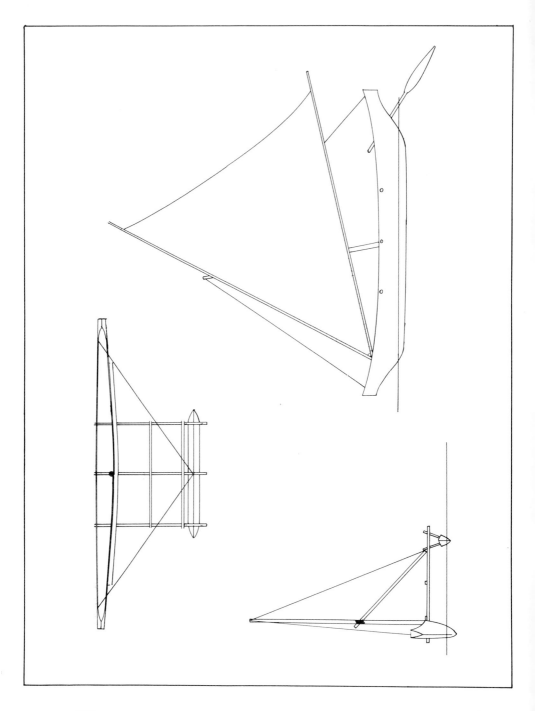

Fig. 11-1. A Micronesian flying proa.

problem which we shall examine presently. Another problem occurred
in that the two masts carrying high aspect fully battened sails were
placed too close together and the foresail had a marked tendency to
backwind the main at speed.

Proas, being the laterally asymmetrical craft that they are, are a
natural for the application of leeward Bruce foils. Realizing this,
Cdr. George Chapman, R.N. designed and built the 18 foot hydrofoil
Atlantic proa *Tiger* in 1972. In this craft the long main hull together
with the sail and crew are all to windward. The hydrofoils (two in
number) are mounted on the ends of the tubular crossbeams by 3-foot
struts and have a dihedral angle of 41 degrees. Between the leeward
beam ends is a foam and plywood outrigger of very low buoyancy
to stabilize the boat at low speeds. The sail was a single mainsail
mounted on a rotating mast placed amidships. This craft is shown
schematically in Fig. 11-2. With this arrangement *Tiger* was found to

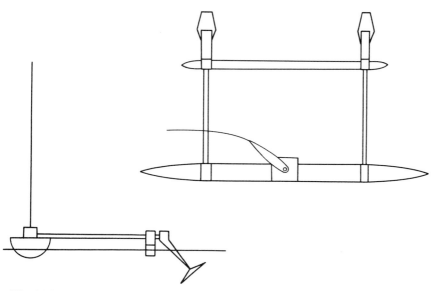

Fig. 11-2. *Tiger* 1972.

have a major flaw concerning helm balance. With the foil angles of
attack set at 5 degrees bow and 4 degrees stern, *Tiger* was balanced,
that is, the yawing torque was zero with the rudder centred only for a
sheeting position just free from close-hauled. Sheeting in produced
weather helm and freeing gave rise to lee helm. The mechanism for
this inbalance is shown in Fig. 11-3. We see from this figure that the
line of action of the sail force F_A only coincides with the line of
action of the resultant hydrodynamic force F_H for one sheeting
position. If the foils are retracted and a leeboard mounted on the
weather hull is used for leeway resistance, then good helm balance
can be maintained over the entire range of sheeting positions. This
discovery accounts for the fact that *Cheers* with its daggerboards in
the windward hull had a much more satisfactory balance than
Sidewinder with its leeway resistors in the lee hull.

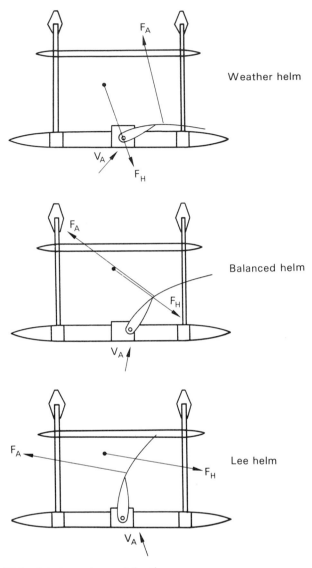

Fig. 11-3. Helm inbalance in an Atlantic proa.

Let us examine this question of balance more thoroughly. In Fig. 11-4 we show the forces acting in a vertical plane on a hydrofoil proa viewed from the leeward side. The equilibrium of vertical and horizontal forces in this profile view gives rise to two equations:

$$F_x = R, \qquad (11\text{-}1)$$

$$\mathscr{L}_S + \mathscr{L}_B = W, \qquad (11\text{-}2)$$

where in writing the latter equation we assume that the boat is operating near its stability limit such that the drag of the windward hull can be neglected. Taking moments about the stern foil and setting the sum of these moments equal to zero gives

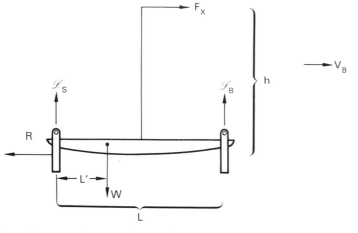

Fig. 11-4. Forces and torques in profile.

$$F_x h + WL' = \mathscr{L}_B L. \tag{11-3}$$

Now let us look at the plan view shown in Fig. 11-5. We assume that the centre of effort of the sail is located a distance b to windward and a distance l forward of the stern foil. Using this figure we find two more equilibrium relations

$$f_S + f_B = F_y, \tag{11-4}$$

and

$$f_B L = F_x b + F_y l. \tag{11-5}$$

If the Bruce foils are to have fixed dihedral angles, (I have spent some time contemplating the engineering possibilities of having

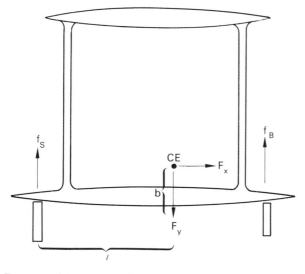

Fig. 11-5. Forces and torques in plan.

variable dihedral angles and, in the end, I rejected the idea as impractical for small craft) then

$$f_{B,S} = \mathscr{L}_{B,S} \tan \theta, \qquad (11\text{-}6)$$

and

$$F_y = W \tan \theta. \qquad (11\text{-}7)$$

In order to solve these equations we need one more relation. Looking at Fig. 6-1 we see that over a reasonably broad range of foil-borne speeds, one may approximate $F_x = R$ by

$$F_x = R \approx \tfrac{1}{7}W \qquad (11\text{-}8)$$

Solving Eqs. (11-1)–(11-8), we find for l, the longitudinal location of the centre of effort

$$l = L' + \tfrac{1}{7}(h - b \operatorname{ctn} \theta) \qquad (11\text{-}9)$$

and for the lifts of the bow and stern foils

$$\mathscr{L}_B = \frac{W}{L}\left(L' + \frac{h}{7}\right), \qquad (11\text{-}10)$$

$$\mathscr{L}s = \frac{W}{L}\left(L - L' - \frac{h}{7}\right). \qquad (11\text{-}11)$$

What does this tell us? If we are considering a proa of such a size that the crew weight can be shifted aft on each tack ($L' < L/2$), then the longitudinal location of the centre of effort can be made to lie aft of the midplane. If, on the other hand we require that the centre of gravity lie in the midplane ($L' = L/2$) as appropriate to a large proa, then for $h > b \operatorname{ctn} \theta$ as required for balance over a wide sheeting range, we find that $l > L/2$ and the centre of effort must lie *forward* of the midplane. This fact must be taken into account in designing the sail rig.

Fig. 11-6.

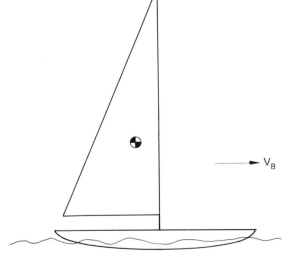

The simplest proa rig might consist of a mast amidships with a unarig as shown in Fig. 11-6. We see, however, that with any such arrangement the centre of effort always lies in the after half of the boat. The sail cannot be mounted so as to move the centre of effort forward of the mast since this would result in an over-balanced arrangement that could not weathercock when the sheet is freed. This leads to the idea of a moveable mast.

In 1973 *Tiger* was redone by mounting a fully battened unarig on the lee hull, that is, the boat was changed from an Atlantic to a Pacific proa. *Tiger* in its 1973 form with the author at the helm is shown in Fig. 6-14. This version was much easier to steer than the earlier Atlantic version. The foot of the rotating mast rides on a track forming an arc of a circle. In performing a shunt, the boat was sailed onto a beam reach. The sheet was released and the mast foot hauled to the midplane. There *Tiger* would lie ahull in a stable manner whilst the steering was rearranged to the other end and the foil angles readjusted. The mast foot was then hauled to the (new) bow and, upon sheeting in, the boat was away on the new tack. The only real complaint with this version was the lack of twist control over the sail.

The moveable mast, à la *Tiger*, is not practical in a large boat. Unless the aspect ratio is very large (lofty rig) or the sail area very low, the centre of effort will not move far enough forward to balance a boat with a midship centre of gravity.

A rig designed by J. S. Taylor in 1962 is shown in Fig. 11-7. The rig uses sails cut in the form of isosceles triangles. Each bottom corner has a multipurchase sheet leading to powerful winches. In the figure the boat is shown moving to the right. The tensioned sheet at the bow acts as the forestay and the stern sheet controls the set of the sail. In shunting, the tensioned sheet is slacked and the slack sheet is tensioned in order to reverse the rig. Clearly this arrangement *will*

Fig. 11-7. The Taylor proa rig.

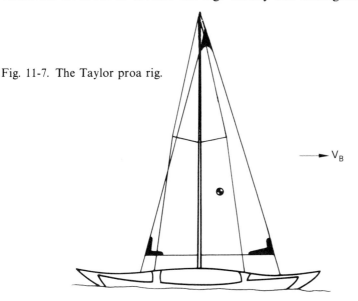

put the centre of effort forward of the mast and is capable of balancing the two Bruce foils. This rig, like any conventional rig with foresails puts a lot of strain on the structure of the boat, however.

In the light of the foregoing, I am inclined to think that a pyramid schooner rig may be the best bet for a large proa. The twin masts and 8 booms will be heavier than the Taylor rig, however the lack of strain transmitted to the hull and connector structure by the pyramid rig should enable the boat to be lighter overall. With a symmetrical schooner rig having its masts far apart, the centre of effort can be adjusted longitudinally over a considerable distance about the mid-plane by playing the sheets. The sails can have fairly high aspect ratio without the rig becoming too lofty. A large variety of reefing combinations are possible without disturbing the balance. Best of all, with two high aspect aerofoils and two high aspect hydrofoils on either end of the boat, it should self-steer as though it were on rails!

The best athwartship location for the rig is to put the centre of effort directly above the line of force of the resultant hydrodynamic drag. Since this condition should be optimized for fast sailing where the drag of the windward hull is reduced, a position on or near the leeward hull is indicated. Thus a non-foil equipped proa can use the Atlantic configuration as *Cheers* did, but a foil-stabilized proa should be of the Pacific type.

It should be noted as previously pointed out in Chapter 6 that the heeling elimination relation Eq. (6-7) is satisfied for *any* athwartship location of the sail as long as the line of action of the hydrofoil force intersects the line of action of the sail force directly above the centre of gravity. It is this condition that Eq. (6-7) implies and not the more restrictive condition that the line of action of the hydrofoil pass through the sail at the centre of effort.

In any seagoing system, simplicity is a cardinal virtue. In accordance with this philosophy, it is suggested that the Bruce foils be fixed with their struts in the vertical position so that the only adjustment possible is full retraction. In order that the bow foil automatically have higher lift coefficients than the stern for either direction of travel, the bottom rung of the foils will be fixed at a 0° angle of attack, the second rung at $+1.3°$ bow, $-1.3°$ stern; the third at $+2.6°$ bow, $-2.6°$ stern; and the top rungs at $+4°$ and $-4°$. This arrangement always gives the bow more lift than the stern in either direction and does not require adjustment during a shunt. Any perturbation that causes the bow to pitch down will cause the lift to decrease more rapidly at the stern. Thus a positive angle of attack at the bow is quickly restored.

Fig. 11-8. Foil rudders.

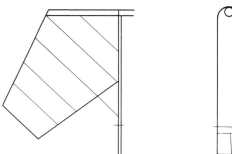

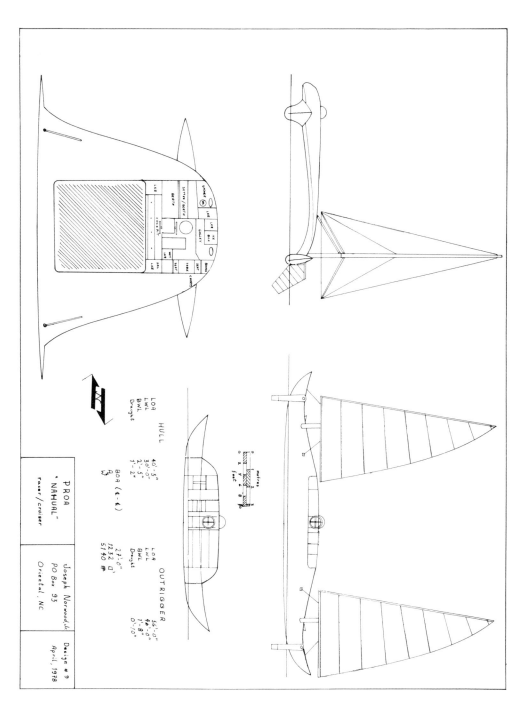

Fig. 11-9. An offshore hydrofoil proa schooner.

What about steering? In Chapt. 5 we discussed several steering systems that might be applied to a proa and concluded that the use of double-acting spade rudders at the bottom of the leeboards appeared feasible. These leeboards can be adjusted vertically in daggerboard cases mounted on the windward side of the lee hull so as to balance the boat with the helm amidship. The cases are normally locked in the vertical position by a mechanical 'fuse' that will allow the boards to swing up in either direction if struck by the ground or a floating log. In a foil-borne proa, these rudders can be mounted in the bottom of the foils as shown in Fig. 11-8. Since the foils must be capable of being retracted for shallow water or light-air sailing, the steering linkage is best done with hydraulics. For such conditions steering can be done by a system such as that shown in Fig. 5-11.

The result of these deliberations in the form of a conceptual design for a modern offshore proa is shown in Fig. 11-9. The differences in a proa and a catamaran or trimaran are such that we must begin to build such craft before we will have all the little problems sorted out. As an example of one 'little problem' for which the author has already found a cure, consider how to move the lubber line 180 degrees around the compass when going on the other tack. The solution is to buy a compass set in double gimbals. By inverting the compass about both axes as shown in Fig. 11-10, the lubber line ends up on the opposite side.

REFERENCES

1 Chapman, George, AYRS *Airs*, *4*, 18 (1972).

2 Follett, Tom, Dick Newick, and Jim Morris, *Project Cheers*, London: Adlard Coles, Ltd., 1969.

3 Haddon, A. C., and James Hornell, *Canoes of Oceania*. Honolulu, Hawaii: Bishop Museum Press, Reprinted 1975.

4 Herreshoff, L. Francis, *The Common Sense of Yacht Design*. Jamaica, N.Y.: Caravan-Maritime Books, 1974.

5 Hughes, Chris, AYRS, *68*, 13 (1969).

6 Morwood, John, AYRS, *71*, 70 (1970).

7 Norwood, Joseph, AYRS *Airs*, *8*, 76 (1974).

8 Norwood, Joseph, AYRS *Airs*, *9*, 46 (1975).

9 Norwood, Joseph, *Multihulls*, *2*, 62 (Winter 1976).

10 Norwood, Joseph, *Some Thoughts on the Ultimate Yacht*, MIAPH-GP-72.4, University of Miami, 1972.

11 Taylor, J. S., AYRS, *71*, 80 (1970).

12 AYRS, *75*, 81 (1971).

13 AYRS, *1*, 13 (1956).

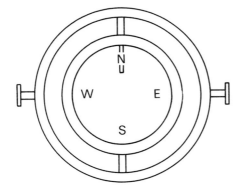

(1) Rotate 180° about NS axis

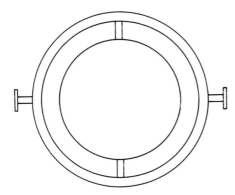

(2) Rotate 180° about EW axis

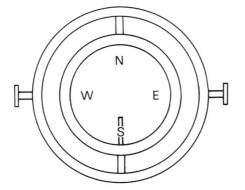

Fig. 11-10. Compass reversal.

117

12 AN OVERALL VIEW

On any course save dead downwind, the speed of a sailing boat with respect to the true wind speed is determined by β, the angle between the velocity vector of the boat and the apparent wind vector. The smaller β, the faster the boat. The course theorem Eq. (1-5) shows us that β can be thought of as the sum of two angles, the aerodynamic and hydrodynamic drag angles, which in turn depend on the lift-to-drag ratio of the above water and below water parts of the boat respectively. The problem to be solved in designing a fast sailing boat is just the problem of maximizing these lift-to-drag ratios for all conditions of sailing in a manner consistent with seaworthiness of the boat and the necessary comforts for the crew.

The hydrodynamic drag angle for *any* sailing boat (ice yachts excepted) is much larger than its aerodynamic drag angle for all useful courses (full and by as opposed to pinched). By far the dominant component of the hydrodynamic drag is that due to the running resistance of the hull. It is therefore vital to know how to minimize the running resistance of the hull for a given load-carrying ability. We found that Castles approximation to Havelock's wave resistance theory gives us this information in a very general way. Using this relation we are able to show that hulls and outriggers should be designed with the highest possible prismatic coefficient consistent with a clean (that is, non-eddy producing) entry. As a means for doing this in practice, we note that a 14 degree half angle of entry has been found empirically to be very nearly ideal. If one therefore imposes this condition, then for the high length to beam ratios of interest, appropriately high prismatics will result.

My recommendation with regard to trimaran outriggers is unconventional. At present designers are divided between favouring full buoyancy and low buoyancy (submersible) outriggers. It seems to me that since the lee outrigger carries a large portion of the weight of the boat in windward sailing that the overall reduction of drag is best effected by using a full buoyancy outrigger with as low a DLR as overall weight considerations and the current state of building materials permits. In general the outrigger should be somewhat longer than the hull. I should expect this approach to yield a boat that can slide sideways on a steep wave without tripping and still have the freedom from jerky roll motion featured by present low buoyancy designs.

The present state of the art of boat building and materials technology allows very light, highly extended structures to be contemplated. One cannot overbuild a racing multihull in the same way that one would with a cruising monohull. We must be aware however that the beam-to-hull connections and the boards, rudders, and hydrofoils are subject to prodigious forces. These areas should be designated for the use of exotic materials such as Kevlar and carbon fibres. Avoid the use of Kevlar under compression; experience has shown that it fails very easily under such conditions.

The lowest possible aerodynamic drag angle can be achieved with the use of a well designed light-weight wingsail. It seems likely that these devices will dominate C-class catamaran racing in the near future. For larger ocean-going craft, the complication and difficulty in reducing sail proclude the use of wingsails. Another approach to low δ_A is to use a very large sail area. Since the amount of sail that can be carried by a given hull arrangement with a given weight distribution is an inverse function of h, the height of the centre of effort, one is led to consider distributing the sail area laterally. Laterally divided rigs have been seen on various speed record machines including *Crossbow II* and *Clifton Flasher*. The simplest way of mounting two sails laterally with minimal spar lengths and windage is the pyramid rig. This rig, heretofore untried for high performance craft, offers many practical advantages for offshore sailing. Jack Manners-Spencer has been promoting its use in England for some time with only limited success. The pyramid rig is an excellent rig with many virtues and deserves to catch on.

The sailing efficiency of a fast boat is dependent on having an optimal value of the keel area for a given sail area and course angle. Thus some type of variable area keel must be contemplated. The choices are effectively limited to centreboards, daggerboards, and leeboards. Regardless of the fact that they have seldom been seen on racing multihulls, leeboards seem to have the best of the argument when compared with the other two choices. Surface ventilation, the only real problem with leeboards, can be prevented by raking them forward and by using a twisted board such that the immersed part has about 4° more angle of attack than the waterline. Helicopter blades are discarded long before their useful life is done, and can be used to make very good leeboards. In the few cases where leeboards have been used in a high-speed application, as for example, on the Gougeon trimaran *Funkey*, they have worked quite well. If we consider the nature of inherent self-steering ability, an extremely important property of any offshore racer, we find that the lateral plane should best be divided between two high aspect plates located near the bow and stern respectively. If one uses a skeg/rudder combination with a reasonable portion of area in the skeg together with a leeboard forward and a low aspect rig or one that is divided longitudinally, good self-steering properties result.

The era of offshore sailing hydrofoils is not yet with us, but we can be fairly certain that we are on the brink of it. Trimarans and proas in particular lend themselves to an advantageous use of hydrofoils for drag reduction, heeling cancelation, and improved seakindliness. Past efforts in this direction have underestimated the design criteria and have not realized the maximum potential advantages, *Mayfly* and *Williwaw* excepted. All that one needs to do the job right is included in this book and I hope that the next generation of fast sailing craft will take full advantage.

Public resistance to multihulls largely centres around the fear of capsize. Previous efforts to devise a scheme to right a capsized multi-hull the same way it went over, namely sideways, have not met with success. An over-the-bows scheme recently put forth by C. J. Ruiz looks like a winner, however. It is hoped that offshore tests being planned at the time of this writing will be carried to fruition by the time this book appears and multihullers will be able to hold their heads high at any gathering of yachtsmen.

Francis Herreshoff said it all when he said that the pleasure in sailing is directly proportional to the speed attained.

Good sailing.

APPENDIX A
DERIVATION OF THE HAVELOCK-CASTLES EQUATION

In a series of papers published in the Proceedings of the Royal Society between 1909 and 1932, T. H. Havelock examined the problem of wave resistance from a basic point of view. His method was to replace the hull by a collection of fluid sources in the forward part and sinks in the stern part. The strength of these sources and sinks is specified such that the resulting flow about them is just equivalent to the flow about the actual hull. If ζ is the surface elevation above the unperturbed surface, then the generalized (for unsteady motions) Bernoulli equation gives for the pressure condition at the free surface

$$\frac{\partial \Phi}{\partial t} - g\zeta + \mu\Phi = \text{const.} \tag{A-1}$$

where Φ is the velocity potential, g is the acceleration of gravity and μ is the coefficient of friction where the friction force is assumed to be proportional to the velocity. This friction term is introduced as a computational device and is later set equal to zero, thus its inclusion does not amount to a restriction on the generality of the results. (Later workers have shown that wave drag can also be derived without including the friction term. See, for example, J. J. Stoker, *Water Waves*. New York: Interscience Publishers, Inc., 1957.) Since $\partial\zeta/\partial t$ is just the z-component of fluid velocity and ζ must satisfy a wave equation

$$\frac{\partial^2 \Phi}{\partial t^2} = V_B{}^2 \frac{\partial^2 \Phi}{\partial x^2}, \tag{A-2}$$

thus Eq. (A-1) can be recast as

$$\frac{\partial^2 \Phi}{\partial x^2} + \frac{g}{V_B{}^2} \frac{\partial \Phi}{\partial z} - \frac{\mu}{V_B} \frac{\partial \Phi}{\partial x} = 0 \tag{A-3}$$

Havelock then writes a general expression for Φ satisfying Eq. (A-3) and including the sources and sinks.

The energy dissipation rate is given by

$$\frac{dE}{dt} = -\mu\rho \iint \Phi \frac{\partial \Phi}{\partial n} dS, \tag{A-4}$$

where ρ is the density of the fluid (sea water), $\partial\Phi/\partial n$ is the derivative normal to the surface, and the integral is taken over the surface of the hull. One now takes the limit as μ approaches zero and finds that dE/dt approaches a finite limit that is identified as the rate at which energy is propagated away by the waves. This power loss is just equal to

$$\lim_{\mu \to 0} \frac{dE}{dt} = R_W V_B \qquad \text{(A-5)}$$

where R_W is the wave drag. The result is given by

$$R_W = \frac{16\pi\rho g}{V_B^2} \int_0^{\pi/2} (P_e^2 + P_0^2 + Q_e^2 + Q_0^2)\sec^3\theta \, d\theta \qquad \text{(A-6)}$$

where

$$P_e = \int \alpha e^{-kz} \cos(kx \cos\theta)\cos(ky \sin\theta) \, dS,$$

$$P_0 = \int \alpha e^{-kz} \sin(kx \cos\theta)\sin(ky \sin\theta) \, dS,$$

$$\qquad\qquad\qquad\qquad\qquad\qquad\qquad\qquad\qquad\qquad\text{(A-7)}$$

$$Q_e = \int \alpha e^{-kz} \sin(kx \cos\theta)\cos(ky \sin\theta) \, dS,$$

$$Q_0 = \int \alpha e^{-kz} \cos(kx \cos\theta)\sin(ky \sin\theta) \, dS;$$

α is the density of sources and sinks and

$$k = \frac{g}{V_B^2} \sec^2\theta. \qquad \text{(A-8)}$$

If the hull has lateral symmetry, then $P_0 = Q_0 = 0$; if longitudinal symmetry also obtains, then $Q_e = 0$.

Equations (A-6) and (A-7), interesting though they are, still do not tell us how to design hulls. This problem was solved by Walter Castles who suggested using a single source in the bow and a corresponding sink in the stern. If we take a coordinate system moving with the hull such that x is the longitudinal coordinate, y is the lateral coordinate, and z is the vertical coordinate with the origin located symmetrically in the mid-plane, then the prismatic coefficient can be defined as

$$C_P = \frac{\nabla}{\sigma L} = \frac{x_{\text{source}} - x_{\text{sink}}}{L}. \qquad \text{(A-9)}$$

For a single hull we then take $x = C_P(L/2)$, $y = 0$, $z = \delta$ where δ is the depth of the centroid of the maximum cross section σ. Plugging this assumption back into Eqs. (A-6) and (A-7), one finds after some algebra

$$R_W = \tfrac{1}{2}\rho V_B^2 \left(\frac{\sigma}{L}\right)^2 C_W \qquad \text{(A-10)}$$

where

$$C_W = \frac{4}{\pi F^4} \int_0^{\pi/2} \left[1 - \cos\left(\frac{C_P}{F^2} \sec \theta\right)\right] \exp\left(-\frac{2\delta}{F^2} \sec^2 \theta\right) \sec^3 \theta \, d\theta$$

(A-11)

For the purpose of numerical integration, the nonconstant period of the cosine is bothersome, hence we make the following change in variables. Let

$$x = \frac{C_P}{F^2} \sec \theta$$

(A-12)

Equation (A-11) then becomes

$$C_W = \frac{4}{\pi C_P^2} \int_{x_0}^{\infty} (1 - \cos x) \frac{x^2 e^{-ax^2}}{\sqrt{x^2 - x_0^2}} \, dx$$

(A-13)

where

$$x_0 = \frac{C_P}{F^2}; \qquad a = \frac{2\delta}{L} \left(\frac{F}{C_P}\right)^2.$$

(A-14)

For the case of a catamaran, a two-source, two-sink approximation may be used in which $x = C_P(L/2)$, $y = \pm(b/2)$ where b is the centreline to centreline hull spacing. One then finds for C_W

$$C_W = \frac{2}{\pi C_P^2} \int_{x_0}^{\infty} (1 - \cos x)[1 + \cos(\beta x \sqrt{x^2 - x_0^2})] \frac{x^2 e^{-ax^2}}{\sqrt{x^2 - x_0^2}} \, dx$$

(A-15)

where $\beta = b/x_0$. It can be seen that Eq. (A-15) reduces to (A-13) for $b = 0$. The integrand of Eq. (A-15) is indetermininent at its lower limit $x = x_0$; this limit must be evaluated from Eq. (A-13) and one finds

$$y_0 = 2x_0^2(1 - \cos x_0)e^{-ax_0^2}.$$

(A-16)

In integrating numerically, one integrates cycle by cycle using Simpson's rule. The integration can be cut off when the increment from the last cycle is less than one percent of the total. The first cycle $x = x_0$ to $x = x_0 + 2\pi$ should be divided into at least 64 increments. The number of increments can then be halved on each succeeding cycle until four increments are reached. For the purpose of checking the calculation, the following data are given for Castles' catamaran:

$$\nabla = 87.5 \text{ ft}^3 \qquad V_B = 7 \text{ knots}$$
$$\sigma = 4 \text{ ft}^2 \qquad \delta = 0.55 \text{ ft.}$$
$$L = 29.3 \text{ ft.} \qquad b = 10 \text{ ft.}$$
$$R_W = 148.2 \text{ lbs.}$$

APPENDIX B
HULL RESISTANCE FOR
SEMICIRCULAR SECTIONS

Hull resistance for semicircular sections using the Havelock-Castles equation for $L = 25$ ft, $V_B = 10$ kts.

DLR	L/B	C_P	R_f/W	R_W/W	R/W	W	R, lb.	W/R
60	9.66	.5	.0326	.0712	.1038	2100	218.0	9.63
60	10.1	.55	.0309	.0613	.0922	2100	193.6	10.85
60	10.6	.6	.0297	.0511	.0808	2100	169.7	12.38
60	11.0	.65	.0284	.0438	.0722	2100	151.6	13.85
60	11.4	.7	.0273	.0376	.0649	2100	136.3	15.41
60	11.8	.75	.0263	.0323	.0586	2100	123.1	17.06
60	12.2	.8	.0255	.0276	.0531	2100	111.5	18.83
50	10.6	.5	.0356	.0658	.1014	1750	177.5	9.86
50	11.1	.55	.0338	.0562	.0900	1750	157.5	11.11
50	11.6	.6	.0324	.0466	.0790	1750	138.3	12.66
50	12.1	.65	.0311	.0396	.0707	1750	123.7	14.14
50	12.5	.7	.0298	.0338	.0636	1750	111.3	15.72
50	13.0	.75	.0289	.0283	.0572	1750	100.1	17.48
50	13.4	.8	.0279	.0242	.0521	1750	91.2	19.19
40	11.8	.5	.0395	.0598	.0993	1400	139.0	10.07
40	12.4	.55	.0376	.0505	.0881	1400	123.3	11.35
40	13.0	.6	.0361	.0412	.0773	1400	108.2	12.94
40	13.5	.65	.0346	.0349	.0695	1400	97.3	14.39
40	14.0	.7	.0332	.0296	.0628	1400	87.9	15.92
40	14.5	.75	.0321	.0251	.0572	1400	80.1	17.48
40	15.0	.8	.0311	.0212	.0523	1400	73.2	19.12
35	12.7	.5	.0424	.0559	.0983	1225	120.4	10.17
35	13.3	.55	.0403	.0471	.0874	1225	107.1	11.44
35	13.9	.6	.0385	.0385	.0770	1225	94.3	12.99
35	14.4	.65	.0368	.0328	.0696	1225	85.3	14.37
35	15.0	.7	.0355	.0277	.0632	1225	77.4	15.82
35	15.5	.75	.0343	.0232	.0575	1225	70.4	17.39
35	16.0	.8	.0331	.0197	.0528	1225	64.7	18.94
30	13.7	.5	.0456	.0525	.0981	1050	103.0	10.19
30	14.3	.55	.0432	.0442	.0874	1050	91.8	11.44
30	15.0	.6	.0415	.0358	.0773	1050	81.2	12.94
30	15.6	.65	.0398	.0302	.0700	1050	73.5	14.29

DLR	L/B	C_P	R_f/W	R_W/W	R/W	W	R, lb.	W/R
30	16.2	.7	.0383	.0254	.0637	1050	66.9	15.70
30	16.7	.75	.0368	.0214	.0582	1050	61.1	17.18
30	17.3	.8	.0357	.0180	.0537	1050	56.4	18.62
25	15.0	.5	.0498	.0485	.0983	1050	86.0	10.17
25	15.7	.55	.0473	.0406	.0879	875	76.9	11.38
25	16.4	.6	.0452	.0328	.0780	875	68.3	12.82
25	17.1	.65	.0435	.0275	.0710	875	62.1	14.08
25	17.7	.7	.0418	.0231	.0649	875	56.8	15.41
25	18.3	.75	.0403	.0193	.0596	875	52.2	16.78
25	18.9	.8	.0390	.0163	.0553	875	48.4	18.08
20	16.7	.5	.0553	.0439	.0992	875	69.4	10.08
20	17.6	.55	.0529	.0364	.0893	700	62.5	11.20
20	18.3	.6	.0504	.0293	.0797	700	55.8	12.55
20	19.1	.65	.0485	.0243	.0728	700	51.0	13.74
20	19.8	.7	.0466	.0204	.0670	700	46.9	14.93
20	20.5	.75	.0450	.0171	.0621	700	43.5	16.10
20	21.2	.8	.0436	.0145	.0581	700	40.7	17.21
15	19.3	.5	.0637	.0380	.1017	700	53.4	9.83
15	20.3	.55	.0608	.0314	.0922	525	48.4	10.85
15	21.2	.6	.0582	.0246	.0828	525	43.5	12.08
15	22.0	.65	.0557	.0206	.0763	525	40.1	13.11
15	22.9	.7	.0538	.0171	.0709	525	37.2	14.10
15	23.7	.75	.0520	.0143	.0663	525	34.8	15.08
15	24.4	.8	.0501	.0125	.0626	525	32.9	15.97
10	23.7	.5	.0779	.0291	.1070	350	37.5	9.35
10	24.8	.55	.0741	.0241	.0982	350	34.4	10.18
10	25.9	.6	.0709	.0187	.0896	350	31.4	11.16
10	27.0	.65	.0682	.0154	.0836	350	29.3	11.96
10	28.0	.7	.0656	.0130	.0786	350	26.6	12.72
10	29.0	.75	.0634	.0112	.0746	350	26.1	13.40
10	29.9	.8	.0613	.0099	.0712	350	24.9	14.04

APPENDIX C
THE CONSTANT β YACHT

In Chapt. 8 we showed that polar curves of V_B/V_T versus γ for constant β are circles passing through the origin. Such circles as shown in Fig. C-1 can be described in Cartesian coordinates by the equation

$$(x - x_0)^2 + (y - y_0)^2 = x_0{}^2 + y_0{}^2, \qquad \text{(C-1)}$$

or in polar coordinates ρ, ϕ by

$$\rho = 2\rho_0 \cos(\phi - \phi_0). \qquad \text{(C-2)}$$

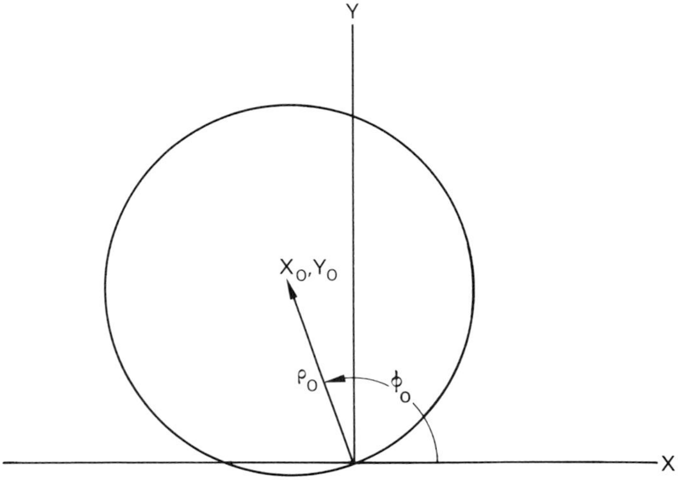

Fig. C-1

Setting $\rho = V_B/V_T$, $\rho_0 = \frac{1}{2} \csc \beta$ [Eq. (8-10)], and $\phi_0 = 90° + \beta$ [Eq. (8-11)], we find

$$\frac{V_B}{V_T} = 2(\tfrac{1}{2} \csc \beta)\cos[\gamma - (90° + \beta)]$$

$$= \csc \beta[\cos \gamma \cos(90° + \beta) + \sin \gamma \sin(90° + \beta)]$$

$$= \csc \beta[\cos \gamma(-\sin \beta) + \sin \gamma \cos \beta]$$

$$= \sin \gamma \operatorname{ctn} \beta - \cos \gamma, \qquad \text{(C-3)}$$

126

the agreement of which with Eq. (8-1) proves the point.

Now we are interested in establishing the course and speed for maximum speed to windward and downwind. The component of V_B/V_T in the windward direction is

$$\left(\frac{V_B}{V_T}\right)_W = \frac{V_B}{V_T}\cos\gamma \qquad (C\text{-}4)$$

and the speed downwind is

$$\left(\frac{V_B}{V_T}\right)_D = -\frac{V_B}{V_T}\cos\gamma \qquad (C\text{-}5)$$

Setting the derivative of $\pm(V_B/V_T)\cos\gamma$ with respect to γ equal to zero to find its maximum value, we obtain the equation

$$\tan 2\gamma = -\operatorname{ctn}\beta, \qquad (C\text{-}6)$$

which has only two roots for γ in the range $0°$ to $180°$

$$\gamma_W = 45° + \frac{\beta}{2}, \qquad (C\text{-}7)$$

and

$$\gamma_D = 135° + \frac{\beta}{2}. \qquad (C\text{-}8)$$

By use of Fig. C-2 we find that the speed made good to windward using the optimal course given by Eq. (C-7) is

$$\left(\frac{V_B}{V_T}\right)_W = \tfrac{1}{2}(\csc\beta - 1) \qquad (C\text{-}9)$$

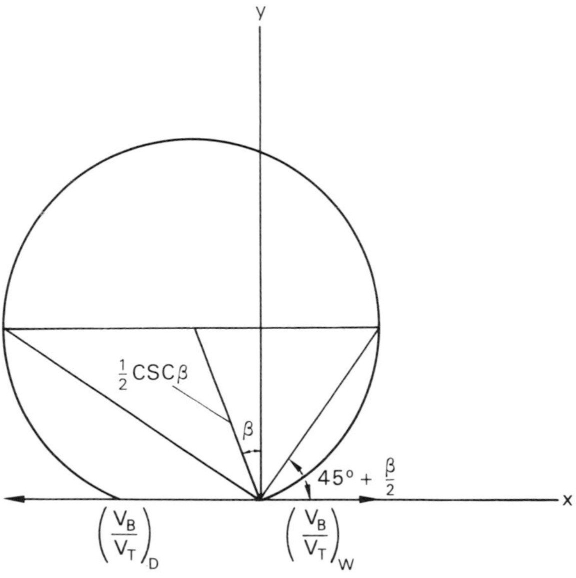

Fig. C-2

and the corresponding speed along the course line is

$$\frac{V_B}{V_T} = \frac{\csc \beta}{2} (\csc \beta - 1). \tag{C-10}$$

The speed made good downwind using the course given by Eq. (C-8) is

$$\left(\frac{V_B}{V_T}\right)_D = \tfrac{1}{2}(\csc \beta + 1), \tag{C-11}$$

and the speed on course is

$$\frac{V_B}{V_T} = \frac{\csc \beta}{2} (\csc \beta + 1). \tag{C-12}$$

A α	Alpha
B β	Beta
Γ γ	Gamma
Δ δ	Delta
E ε	Epsilon
Z ζ	Zeta
H η	Eta
Θ θ	Theta
I ι	Iota
K κ	Kappa
Λ λ	Lambda
M μ	Mu
N ν	Nu
Ξ ξ	Xi
O o	Omicron
Π π	Pi
P ρ	Rho
Σ σ s	Sigma
T τ	Tau
Υ υ	Upsilon
Φ φ	Phi
X χ	Chi
Ψ ψ	Psi
Ω ω	Omega

13

APPENDIX D
LIST OF SYMBOLS USED

Under the constraint of using commonly accepted notation and faced with the large number of symbols required, some ambiguity has been unavoidable. In an effort to avoid confusion each meaning for the various symbols is given along with the number of the equation in which it first appears with that meaning.

SYMBOL	MEANING	FIRST OCCURRENCE
a	beam width	(3-2)
a	proportionality factor	(2-23)
a	strut separation distance	(6-20)
A	aspect ratio	(4-5)
A	cross sectional area of connecting beam	(3-6)
A_F	hydrofoil area	(6-12)
A_K	keel area	(5-2)
A_P	hull area projection on xz plane	(5-5)
A_R	rudder area	(5-11)
A_S	sail area	(4-1)
A_W	wetted surface area of hull	(2-1)
b	lateral distance from CG to CB	(1-7)
b	longitudinal distance between crossbeams	(3-9)
b	lateral distance from CE to CLoR	(11-5)
b	hydrofoil span	(6-20)
B	buoyant force	(6-1)
B	waterline beam	(2-6)
c	chord	(6-14)
C_A	aerodynamic force coefficient	(4-1)
C_D	drag coefficient	(4-3)
C_{Di}	induced drag coefficient	(5-4)
C_F	friction coefficient	(2-1)
C_{Fo}	ideal friction coefficient	(2-4)
C_L	lift coefficient	(4-2)
C_P	prismatic coefficient	(2-17)
C_{PA}	parasitic drag coefficient	(8-6)
C_W	wave resistance coefficient	(2-16)

129

Symbol	Meaning	First Occurrence
C_x	coefficient of longitudinal aerodynamic force	(8-18)
C_y	coefficient of lateral aerodynamic force	(4-9)
CB	centre of buoyancy	
CE	centre of effort of sail	
CG	centre of gravity	
CLaR	centre of lateral resistance	
CLoR	centre of longitudinal resistance	
d	depth of water	
d	separation distance of pyramid sails at CE	(4-12)
d	overall draught (board down)	(5-2)
$\mathscr{D}$	drag	
$\mathscr{D}_A$	aerodynamic drag	(1-6)
$\mathscr{D}_H$	hydrodynamic drag	(1-6)
DLR	displacement-length ratio	(2-22)
E	foil factor	(6-19)
$\mathscr{E}$	deformation energy	(3-8)
F	Froude number	(2-9)
$\mathscr{F}$	hydrofoil lift force	(6-1)
F_A	aerodynamic force	(1-4)
f_B	lateral force of bow foil	(11-4)
F_H	hydrodynamic force	(1-4)
f_S	lateral force of stern foil	(11-4)
F_x	longitudinal component of aerodynamic force	(11-1)
F_y	lateral component of aerodynamic force	(1-7)
g	acceleration of gravity	(2-7)
G	shear modulus	(3-7)
G_m	girth of maximum hull section	(2-20)
h	vertical distance from CE to ClaR	(1-7)
h	half thickness of crossbeam	(3-1)
h	depth of submergence of hydrofoil	(6-14)
H	hull draught	(2-6)
I	areal moment of inertia	(3-1)
k	wave number	(2-10)
K	windward foil depressing force	(6-9)
l	crossbeam length	(3-1)
l	longitudinal distance from stern foil to CE	(11-5)
L	waterline length	(2-2)
L	longitudinal distance between stern and bow foils	(11-3)
L'	longitudinal distance from stern foil to CG	(11-3)
$\mathscr{L}$	lift	
$\mathscr{L}_A$	aerodynamic lift	(1-6)
$\mathscr{L}_B$	vertical force of bow foil	(11-2)

130

Symbol	Meaning	First Occurrence
$\mathscr{L}_H$	hydrodynamic lift	(1-6)
$\mathscr{L}_S$	vertical force of stern foil	(11-2)
N	torque, moment of force	(4-7)
r	radius	(3-4)
R	total resistance	(2-23)
Re	Reynold's number	(2-2)
R_F	frictional resistance	(2-1)
R_i	induced resistance	(5-5)
R_W	wave resistance	(2-13)
S	span	(4-5)
SLR	speed-length ratio	
t	time	(A-1)
V_A	apparent wind speed	(1-1)
V_B	boat speed	(1-1)
V_T	true wind speed	(1-1)
V_W	wave speed	(2-8)
W	boat weight	(1-7)
x	longitudinal coordinate	(2-10)
y	lateral coordinate	
$\bar{y}$	lateral distance from ClaR to CG	(4-7)
$\bar{y}'$	lateral distance from windward foil to ClaR	(6-9)
z	vertical coordinate	(2-10)
$\bar{z}$	vertical distance from ClaR to CG	(4-7)
α	density of sources and sinks	(A-7)
α	angle of attack	
α_T	angle of attack measured from zero lift	(4-6)
β	course angle to apparent wind velocity	(1-2)
γ	course angle to true wind velocity	(1-2)
δ	depth of centroid of largest hull section	(2-18)
δ	camber	
Δ	displacement in tons	
∇	displacement volume	(A-9)
δ_A	aerodynamic drag angle	(1-5)
δ_H	hydrodynamic drag angle	(1-5)
ε	ratio of parasitic area to sail area	(8-6)
ζ	wave amplitude	(2-7)
η	viscosity	(2-2)
θ	heel angle	(4-7)
θ	dihedral angle	(6-1)
κ	foil factor	(6-14)
λ	wavelength	(2-8)
λ	leeway angle	(5-1)
μ	friction coefficient	(A-1)
ν	weight density	(9-5)
ν_1	speed factor	(8-18)
ν_2	stability factor	(8-24)
ρ_A	mass density of air	(4-1)

131

Symbol	Meaning	First Occurrence
ρ_H	mass density of water	(2-1)
σ	foil factor	(6-17)
σ	area of largest hull section	(2-16)
σ_{max}	maximum strain	(3-1)
τ	skin thickness	(3-3)
ϕ	sweep angle	(6-22)
Φ	velocity potential	(A-1)
ϕ	torsion angle	(3-7)
ψ	sail slope angle	(4-12)
Ψ	constant	(8-8)
Ω	foil factor	(6-15)

INDEX